PERSPECTIVES ON THE JACK TALES

AND

OTHER NORTH AMERICAN MÄRCHEN

Special Publications of the Folklore Institute No. 6

Special Publications of the Folklore Institute is published at Indiana University with the editorial guidance of the Folklore Institute Faculty. This series provides a flexible forum for the occasional publication of reports on current research, field data, bibliographies, course readings, and other materials of interest to the broad folkloristic community.

This edited collection was originally published as a special issue of the *Journal of Folklore Research*, Vol. 38, Nos. 1 and 2 (January–August 2001).

John McDowell *Special Publications Editor*
Inta Gale Carpenter *Special Publications Associate Editor*
Mary Ellen Brown *Journal of Folklore Research Editor*
Danille Christensen Lindquist *Journal of Folklore Research Editorial Assistant*

Perspectives on the Jack Tales

AND OTHER NORTH AMERICAN MÄRCHEN

EDITED BY CARL LINDAHL

THE FOLKLORE INSTITUTE / INDIANA UNIVERSITY BLOOMINGTON

Library of Congress Cataloging-in-Publication Data

A catalog record for this book is available
from the Library of Congress.

ISBN 1-878318-75-6

Text Design and Composition by CompuType, Bloomington
Cover Design by inari, Bloomington
Distributed by Indiana University Press,
Bloomington and Indianapolis

Printed in the United States of America

Dedicated to the memory

of

H ERBERT H ALPERT

[August 23, 1911 – December 29, 2000]

for six decades an avid champion and

scholar of British- and Irish-American Märchen

Herbert Halpert recording a version of "The King of Cats" from James L. Conklin, New York, 1946. *Photographed by Violetta Maloney Halpert.*

Contents

Foreword

THIS VOLUME IS ABOUT North American Märchen, and the tales of necessity take pride of place. Interspersed throughout are examples of a vernacular art that has been strangely ignored or misconstrued, but whose vitality and portability into a textualized world (often in highly edited form) attest to its persistent appeal. Though recorded on the printed page, these narratives continue to live orally—especially in the private realm—as one splendid mechanism of intergenerational communication or as symbolic articulation of worldview.

The body of work printed herein grew out of research presented at "American Magic: The Fates of Oral Fiction in the New World," a conference held at the University of Houston in October 1997. In addition to four interpretive essays, six segments feature narrators and their transcribed narratives, accompanied by contextualizing introductions. Some of these segments compare editing practices or narrative styles; others represent the first publication of contemporary narratives or tales that have long lain in archives, unheard and unavailable. In his substantial introductory essay, editor Carl Lindahl suggests the illustrative aim of each narrative section and also explains the terms and transcription techniques used throughout. Section titles point to the issues raised by each narrative or set of narratives; the tales themselves—and the artists who created them—remain the primary focus.

For yet another perspective on some of these tellers and their tales, readers may visit the *Journal of Folklore Research* online at http://www.indiana.edu/~jofr. Video and audio clips of tale performances are available in the section entitled "multimedia features."

—Mary Ellen Brown
Indiana University

A Tale of Verbal Economy: "Stiff Dick"

Samuel Harmon told "Stiff Dick" near Maryville, Tennessee, April 27, 1939; the tale was recorded by Herbert Halpert for the Archive of American Folk Song and is currently housed in the Archive of Folk Culture, American Folklife Center, Library of Congress (recordings AFS 2924B, 2925A).

"Stiff Dick" and the other tales told by Sam Harmon are notable in several respects. They represent the earliest British-American Märchen recordings currently housed in the Archive of Folk Culture, and I have found no earlier recordings anywhere. Furthermore, these tales represent the earliest sound recordings of America's most celebrated Märchen-telling family: the Hicks-Harmon family, whose members include Jane Gentry, Maud Long, and Ray Hicks. (For more information on these storytellers, see the Introduction and the essay "Sounding a Shy Tradition," this volume.) Finally, because Sam Harmon belonged to the same extended family that provided Richard Chase with many of the stories that appear in Chase's *The Jack Tales* (1943), Harmon's performances offer the best available evidence for gauging the extent to which Chase's published versions altered the Hicks-Harmon storytelling tradition. Readers who compare Sam Harmon's and Richard Chase's versions of the same family tale will find enormous differences between the two performances. "Stiff Dick," for example, is nearly identical in plot to "Jack and the Varmints" (Chase 1943:58–66), which Chase stitched together from performances by four members of the Hicks-Harmon family living in North Carolina: Sam's first cousins R. M. Ward and Miles Ward, as well as two more distant relatives (Chase 1943:192).

Herbert Halpert recorded "Stiff Dick" in the context of two lengthy visits at the home of Sam's son, Austin Harmon. Halpert had come to collect folksongs and instrumental performances from father and son. Only at the beginning of the sixth day of Halpert's second visit did Sam begin to tell him tales. Although Halpert saved written notes on his recording sessions with the Harmon family and offered observations on various comments made by family members when the recording machine was not running (Halpert 1939:22, 47, 59–62), he did not record the precise context of the performance of "Stiff Dick" nor did he offer any written observations on Sam's performance style. When I met with Halpert in 1994 and asked him about Sam Harmon's tales, he was distressed that he could not remember the session well enough to

1

offer an evaluation. In 1997, having listened to the 1939 recordings housed in the American Folklife Center, I transcribed "Stiff Dick" and some other Harmon tales and sent copies of my transcriptions to Halpert, who responded that he was "delighted" that the tales were finally being transcribed. On the basis of what he had read, Halpert offered an incisive comment about Harmon: "I'm impressed by what an economically efficient storyteller he was" (personal correspondence, March 26, 1997).

"Economically efficient" precisely sums up Harmon's performance and denotes its major points of contrast with Richard Chase's published text of "Jack and the Varmints." Harmon's tale requires fewer than 1200 words; Chase's runs to more than 2200. Most of Chase's additions function to characterize Jack as boastful and verbose. For example, in the final episode of Chase's version, Jack falls from a tree onto the back of a lion that he has been trying to escape. The lion runs into town with Jack on its back, and the king's men shoot it. Then, in Chase's words:

> *The king came along right soon and Jack says to him, says, "Look-a-here, King. I'm mad."*
> *"Why, how come, Jack?"*
> *"These men have done killed your lion."*
> *"My lion? What ye mean, Jack?"*
> *"Why, I'd 'a not had it killed for three thousand dollars, King. After I'd caught it and 'gun to get it gentled up, now, bedads, your men have done shot it. I was just a-ridin' it down here to get it broke in for you a ridey-horse."*
> *So the old King went over to where his men were and raised a rumpus with 'em, says, "Why, I'd 'a felt big ridin' that lion around. Now you men will just have to raise Jack three thousand dollars for killin' our lion."*
> *So Jack went on home after that; had a whole pile of money down in his old ragged overhall pocket.*
> *And the last time I went down there Jack was still rich, and I don't think he's worked any yet. (1943:66)*

Chase has expended 163 words on this scene; Harmon's parallel scene, by contrast, requires only 27:

> *And Jack said, "Now," he said, "you have to pay me another thousand dollars." Says, "I'm just a breaking this lion," said, "for the king's riding horse."*

In contrast to Chase's cagey rhetorician, Harmon's Jack makes his point with very few words, yet they are sufficient to convert a situation of fear into an economic and moral victory for the boy, who has the last word in the tale and gives it a punch-line ending.

Although Sam Harmon and his hero use their words sparingly, they use them to great effect. In just over 50 percent of the verbiage that Chase devotes to his parallel tale, Sam Harmon renders a remarkably full portrait of a poor orphan boy motivated by both need and fear. Harmon presents Jack's economic status and social context much more fully than Chase does. Thus, not only in terms of verbiage, but also in terms of characterization and motivation, Harmon's economy offers a powerful contrast to Chase's prolix and wasteful style, which presents Jack as a study in undermotivated cleverness. (For a more lengthy discussion of these and other differences between Harmon's version of "Stiff Dick" and Chase's "Jack and the Varmints," see "Sounding a Shy Tradition.")

It may seem paradoxical to state that Sam Harmon's delivery is both lively and understated. Compared to the Märchen-telling styles of his North Carolina relatives Maud Long (Library of Congress LPs 47 and 48) and Ray Hicks (*Ray Hicks of Beech Mountain, North Carolina, Telling Four Traditional "Jack Tales,"* Folk-Legacy Records, 1963), Sam's performance displays little variation in pitch or volume. He speaks quickly and often runs his sentences together; nevertheless, he clearly conveys the motions of the plot through the crispness of his vocabulary. There is a certain detached impersonality about his performance. Sam chuckles in delight at the end of the tale, as though he were its audience rather than its teller, and as though the collector were present merely to overhear Sam Harmon *telling himself* this tale.

Carl Lindahl
University of Houston

"Stiff Dick"
as told by Samuel Harmon, April 27, 1939

One time this orphan boy raised up, he just made what he made out of hisself. His mother wasn't much, and he had no father and he just roved here and yonder everywhere til he got—he got to be a young man.

And he's a going along one day, traveling, he didn't know where he was at. He was way out in a strange country, he didn't know whereabouts he's at or nothing.

And [it's] summer time; he had him a paddle. Walking along where the cat had been and this, this—seven of these big old green flies a settin. And he upped his paddle and killed seven at the lick. He traveled on and—then he went and had a buckle put on his belt and had it printed on his buckle,

Stiff Dick:
Killed Seven at a Lick.

First thing he knowed, he rambled around, got to the king's house, and he went in and stayed til dinner and so pulled his belt off and laid it on the bed when he went in to dinner. And the king, he got done eating and went out, and he happened to notice this on his belt. When he got done eating, he come out, he said, "You must be a terrible warrior." Says, "Here it is on your belt, 'Stiff Dick: Killed Seven at a Lick.'"

Said, bedad, he was.

Says, "You're the very man I've been looking, looking for for years." Says, "I've got a, got a job for you."

He want to know what it was.

"Well," he says, "there's a unicorn and a lion and a wild boar in these woods that destroyed—no telling the people and stock that they destroyed. I never could run acrost no man brave enough to destroy em—til you."

"Ah," he said, "bedad," he said, he would.

He says, "I'll give you a thousand dollars for the boar, a thousand dollars for the unicorn, and a thousand dollars for the lion." Said, "I'll pay you five hundred down and the other thousand when you bring em in."

He told em, Jack told him, that it was alright.

He paid him five hundred dollars, just pleased the poor boy to death, you know—he never did have no money, and he thinks now he'll slip around and get out of there and not run across him. He's easing through the woods and got away out in the forest and the unicorn out in the side of the mountain, here they come—just as hard as they could run and took after Jack, and Jack just run as hard as he could run and he come to a big oak tree. And he got to running around that tree and the unicorn after him (and the unicorn just had one straight horn in its forehead, right out this way) and he's jabbing at him and at last he made a big lunge and jabbed his horn into that tree and couldn't pull it out.

Jack, he got him a little hickory and he reached around the tree and [looked], you know, to see if he could get loose, and seed he's fast. Goes on back to the king's house and—

"Well," the king said, "did you get him, Jack?"

"Get him?" He said he'd never seed nothing to get. He said, hisself, he's a going out there through the woods, said a little old bull come yelling, come busting out there. And he picked up the end of the tail, stove his horn in that tree out there. "If you want to kill it, go kill it."

Well, the king sent a fellow out there and shot it and paid Jack the other five hundred. That made him a thousand.

And there's a wild boar, the next one he's a going to get. So he made sure he'd get out that time. He had all the money he thought he'd ever need. And so there's an old big log house out in the forest and where the campers used to stay, and the roof had about rottened off, all of it, and he's a going along, and the old wild boar heard him. And here they come a bellowing, and Jack broke into a run and as hard as he could fly and he just did get in the old house—before the hog got him, he clumb up on the joists.

The hog—he run in the house. He's hot and tired and he laid down, and he went to sleep, the old hog did, and Stiff Dick—Jack— he slipped around and eased down and shut the door and shut him up out there and eased out while the hog's asleep. And goes back to the king's house and says—

The king says, "Well, did you get him, Jack?"

"Ah," says, "Get him?" He said he didn't see nothing to get. He says he's going out there through the woods, said a little old boar shoat come bristling at him, said he picked up the tail in the air, he said, and pitched in it that old house out there. Said, "If you want to kill it, go out there and kill it."

The king, he sent a fellow out there and shot it. And they paid him his other five hundred. That made him two thousand.

The lion was yet to get. He just knowed in his own mind that he'd get around that lion and not find it out. He started and traveled on and begin to think he's out of reach of the lion, [but] about between sundown and dark the lion found him out.

Here they come. Jack, he run up a tree. And the lion, he went to gnawing the tree. He gnawed the tree and gnawed, kept gnawing— had the tree until it was weaving backwards and forwards. Just about daylight, the old lion got so tired and sleepy and he just laid down beneath the tree and went to sleep.

And Jack thought: now, whiles he's asleep. He'd ease down and get away while the lion is asleep. He kept clumbin on down, clumbin on down—he got down. There's a dead limb on the tree about ten foot above the lion and he got down and went to get down that dead limb to peep over, to see if the lion's eyes—he was well, good asleep.

He stepped on that limb. And the limb broke and fell right astraddle the lion and he wound his hands in this wood and went to hollering and screaming as hard as he could scream and got the lion excited and [chuckling] the lion went to him just as hard as he could fly through the woods.

And he happened to run right through the king's yard. And the king demanded to run out and shoot him quick. And they run out and shot the lion. And Jack said, "Now," he said, "you have to pay me another thousand dollars." Says, "I'm just a breaking this lion," said, "for the king's riding horse." [chuckles]

That's all of it.

Carl Lindahl

Introduction: Representing and Recovering the British- and Irish-American Märchen

"The Man Who Had No Story," a plot best known in Irish and Scottish Gaelic tradition, features a traveler who spends the night at a wayside house in lonely country.

> His host shows him great hospitality, asking in return only one thing, a story. But the visitor cannot remember even one. So the host bears the full burden of the night's entertainment, telling tales nonstop until bedtime. Then, as his host sleeps, the home grows suddenly inhospitable to the visitor. Strangers steal into the house and run off with the host's food. The visitor, fearing he'll be blamed for the theft, pursues the strangers, but loses their trail as he falls into an icy river. He is crying for help, hanging on for dear life to a dangling branch, when he awakes to find himself still in his host's house, clutching a blanket. The host sees him off, saying, "I'm sure that wherever you are tonight, you'll have a story to tell, though you hadn't one last night."[1]

One of the lessons most obviously and frequently drawn from this tale is that those who cannot recall a story are condemned to be the butts of one; another message is that not knowing a story can be, paradoxically, a story in itself. These applications apply equally well to the host of ironies and paradoxes that have clustered around the "non-story" of the British- and Irish-American Märchen.[2] Even as this major oral tradition has been ignored by scholars and exploited by popularizers, it has persisted in living a relatively undisturbed life of its own—a tale of cultural continuity strangely unrecognized by the North American folklore academy, which has become its butt. The North-American Märchen, then, has become the subject of a double-stranded story with an official plot—the academic fiction that

Märchen-telling was dead or dying—as well as a traditional counter-plot: the record of a tenacious living art that has repeatedly belied the experts' claims. Here I consider six of the most pervasive ironies surrounding this two-sided tale.

1) *The earliest documentation of the American Märchen both notes its enormous popularity and declares it dead.* Appropriately, for a genre that situates its actions in the remote "once upon a time," the American Märchen first entered the literary record as a creature whose time, presumably, had already passed. In 1824, even as the Reverend Dr. Joseph Doddridge declared the tales dead, he nevertheless noted their once widespread existence. In the 1760s, as a young boy in what is now West Virginia, Doddridge had heard Märchen performed throughout the frontier:

> Dramatic narrations, chiefly concerning Jack and the Giant, furnished our young people with another source of amusement during their leisure hours. Many of those tales were lengthy, and embraced a considerable range of incident. Jack, always the hero of the story, after encountering many difficulties and performing many great achievements, came off conqueror of the Giant. . . . These dramatic narrations concerning Jack and the Giant bore a strong resemblance to the poems of Ossian, the story of the Cyclops and Ulysses in the Odyssey of Homer, and the tale of the Giant and Great-heart in the Pilgrim's Progress, and were so arranged as to the different incidents of the narration, that they were easily committed to memory. They certainly have been handed down from generation to generation from time immemorial. (1824; cited in Perdue 1987:97)

Doddridge noted that these tales had already been swept away by "civilization," which had "substituted in their place the novel and the romance." If his conclusions were correct, the earliest description of a vital tradition threatened to be the last.

2) But a second irony sprang up: *The Märchen emerged in the scholarly record from the shadows of the genre supposed to have supplanted it—the ballad.* The first generations of American folklorists considered the Märchen, like the ballad, a thing of the past, but as ballads began to resurface and demonstrate their continued lives in tradition, scholars ignored the tales, even as they thrived within their own proximity. The little evidence we have suggests that oral Märchen-telling was rife in the eighteenth century, both in England and in North America. But as the armchair scholars of the late-nineteenth and early-twentieth

centuries found little evidence of Märchen in English-speaking traditions, they developed a genre-shift explanation: the English had channeled their propensity for oral storytelling from prose into poetry,
from Märchen into ballad. Many accepted the English preference for
the ballad as a cultural character trait.

In 1946 Stith Thompson summarized the scholarly consensus,
though not without some healthy doubt:

> Folklorists have always remarked on the scarcity of the authentic folktale
> in England. Popular narrative has had a tendency to take the form of
> the ballad. But there are plenty of evidences, in literature and elsewhere,
> that some of our principal folktales have been current there in the past,
> and the collections made within the last century are not actually so
> meager as usually thought. (19)

Though the ballad was supposed to have run off the folktale, the
Appalachian Märchen was rediscovered—a century after Doddridge
had declared it dead—on the lips of one of the most celebrated Appalachian balladeers of her time, Jane Hicks Gentry of Hot Springs,
North Carolina. The discoverer, Isabel Gordon Carter, accurately re-
marks, "While the collection of ballads has gone steadily on, so far as
the writer knows no collection of the old folk tales has been made in
this region" (1925:340). Carter devoted only two paragraphs to describing the tale teller and her repertoire, but in that short space she
accounted for the presumed rarity of these tales with an explanation
more sound than any other offered before or since:

> At first Mrs. Gentry could not take seriously the writer's request for sto-
> ries. She had given Cecil Sharp and others many of the ballads appear-
> ing in their collections but no one had asked for the stories which she
> had always told to amuse children. (1925:340)

Carter's contextual explanation—that these tales, which served principally to entertain children in intimate family settings, were completely out of place in the formal company of strangers—has been
generally borne out. In 1951, when Leonard Roberts interviewed Dave
Couch of Harlan County, Kentucky, Couch confided his reluctance
to share his tales with outsiders: "We was all kindy skittish about strangers that way. We got the idea they wanted to know our fambly affairs,
or make fun of us" (Roberts 1974:7). Speaking particularly of a group
of women from Berea College who visited him at the Pine Mountain
Settlement School in the early 1900s, Couch remarked, "I was up there

oncet and they wanted me to tell some of my stories. I told 'em one, I told 'em Jack and the Bull Strap, and they took on about it and wanted more. I thought they was making fun, making us out as heathern or something, and I never went back up there and never told 'em another story" (7). In my own fieldwork, I have encountered several tellers who have shared Jim Couch's sense of privacy regarding the magic tale. The intimate, family-based, child-targeted nature of the Appalachian Märchen makes it difficult for most narrators to retell it to adult outsiders. Even willing tellers tend to render the tales only as plot abstracts unless or until children are present, and only then will they actually perform the tales.[3] Ballads, on the other hand, generally are considered more appropriate as public and adult entertainment and have been much more easily collected by folklorists.

The tendency of many informants to hide their tales behind their ballads may have indeed intensified folklorists' bias toward the latter. Yet it is more accurate to say that the ballad has subsumed the Märchen in the minds of folklorists than to assert that it has vanished from the lives of the mountain tellers. Responding either to predetermined ideas that ballads survived and tales did not, or perhaps to the fact that they were successful at collecting ballads and relatively unsuccessful at collecting tales, the major specialists in British-American folklore persisted in studying, publishing, and celebrating ballads. During the first half of the twentieth century, American ballad scholars far outnumbered prose narrative scholars—the students of Francis James Child and their own subsequent students, among others, constituted a formidable company: George Lyman Kittredge, F. B. Gummere, A. K. Davis, Henry Belden, John Lomax, Louise Pound—all dominating names in the field of British- and Irish-American folklore studies.

Five years after Jane Gentry told her tales to Isabel Carter, the bias toward sung narrative was institutionalized at the governmental level by the formation of the Archive of American Folk Song at the Library of Congress, the national repository of recorded folkloric expression. Märchen were indeed collected by the music-minded folklorists and dutifully deposited in the archive, but in every case they were collected from families at least as well known for their singers and musicians. In 1946, Stith Thompson optimistically declared that times were changing: "In the United States the American Folksong Archives [sic] at the Library of Congress is being expanded so as to embrace other aspects of folklore, including the popular tale" (399). Yet, in 1997, more than half a century later, when I visited the American Folklife Center's Archive of Folk Culture (as the Archive of American Folk Song has been renamed), I discovered that the corpus had not been catalogued or evaluated, that the earliest British- and Irish-American Märchen had never been transcribed or published, and that only a handful had been released in recorded form.

Even at the close of the twentieth century, folklorists persisted in tying the tale to the ballad, generally to the detriment of the tale. For example, Michael Ann Williams's survey of Smoky Mountain verbal art, perhaps the best short summary of its kind, nevertheless persists in continuing the connection:

> The telling of Jack tales appears to have strong connections to the ballad-singing tradition. Like ballads, they were performed at home and were maintained through strong family traditions. Generally, traditional Jack tale tellers also shared the deadpan, nonemotional performance style of ballad singers. . . . One suspects . . . that the telling of Jack tales was never quite as widespread as the singing of Child ballads. The fact is that almost all of the traditional Jack tale tellers documented in the North Carolina and Tennessee mountains were descendants of the same man, David Hicks. (1995:115–16)

Williams's analysis is a fine assessment of the evidence on hand—but that evidence was created by a folkloric establishment with a ballad-hunting bias. The one extended family to which Williams refers is the same one to which balladeer Jane Gentry belonged. Most of the Jack tale tellers known to folklorists are also ballad singers, because they too became known to folklore studies by virtue of being ballad singers. But what of those families that have maintained vital narrative—but not ballad or folksong—traditions?[4]

3) *Having "discovered" the British- and Irish-American Märchen, the academic folklore community promptly abandoned the genre to outsiders.* It was not merely a preference for ballads, but an almost unaccountable unwillingness to consider narrative that left its study almost entirely to the incentive of three men. Prior to 1987, all but one of the major books of Märchen from the United States were produced by Vance Randolph, Leonard Roberts, and Richard Chase.[5] Like their

contemporary mainstream folklorists, all three men collected ballads and folksongs. Nevertheless, Randolph, Roberts, and Chase clearly valued the telling of magic tales as a living and major component of American mountain traditional culture, and each of them found ample evidence to support his convictions. Yet all three were, to some extent, outsiders to the folklore establishment.

Vance Randolph (1892–1980), who started earliest and stayed longest in the field, spent sixty years immersed in the largely Appalachian-derived folk culture of the Ozark Mountains of southern Missouri and northern Arkansas. By the end of his prodigious career, he had become an icon to professional folklorists, but his reputation was a long time in the making, and his history of rejection is a long and complex one. Like scholars within the growing discipline of folklore, but less divisively so, Randolph was interested in folk culture equally as art and as social science. But both wings of the folklore establishment placed obstacles in the path of his narrative work. His devotion to folktales found no support among ballad-centered literary folklorists, and his commitment to British-American culture doomed him to rejection by the ethnologists. His earliest attempt at the ethnographic study of oral traditions was a proposal submitted to Franz Boas of Columbia University in 1915. According to Randolph, Boas "was interested in Indians and Eskimos, and blacks. . . . It seemed to me ridiculous. I was interested in white mountain people" (in Cochran 1985:48).

Supporting himself by writing popular pamphlets, Randolph pursued the collection of folktales and folksongs on his own until 1941, when the Archive of American Folk Song loaned him a tape recorder for the collection of songs. Twenty-four more years would pass before he received a comparable honor for his work with folk narrative: *Hot Springs and Hell* (1965) was published by a major folklore press. Randolph would continue to meet rejection or criticism from a host of folklorists in subsequent years. Yet in the end he published six major collections of Ozark oral narratives, four of them rich with Märchen, a body of work unique for this region. Not one substantial additional collection of magic tales from this region has yet emerged (McNeil 1999). Randolph's is, simply, not only the *major* but also effectively the *only* record of what was once a vital British- and Irish-American Märchen-telling community.

For the first three decades of his career in publishing folklore, Randolph placed most of his narrative work in nonacademic venues, for example, in popular pamphlets bearing such titles as *Funny Stories about Hillbillies* (1944).[6] During this period, legends illustrating belief and "superstition"—a more acceptable research topic than Märchen—dominated the types of narrative published in the *Journal of American Folklore* and other leading periodicals. Finally, in 1951, Randolph published "Bedtime Stories from Missouri"—his fifty-fourth folklore publication—in *Western Folklore*, and thus brought two magic tales to print: "Fill, Bowl, Fill" (AT 570) and "The Little Blue Ball" (AT 311). The next year, the floodgates opened with the publication of *Who Blowed Up the Church House?* By the end of the 1950s, three other Märchen-laden collections would see print. Randolph's feats as a collector and scholar of oral prose traditions finally won full recognition in 1978, when at age eighty-six he was named a Fellow of the American Folklore Society.

Of the three major British-American Märchen collectors, Leonard Roberts started last, recording his first tales in 1949, three decades after Randolph. Yet (as one measure of his relative insider position among the three collectors) Roberts's first major published collection, *South from Hell-fer-Sartin* (1955), appeared just three years after Randolph's first. Roberts was the most orthodoxly educated of the three folklorists: he attended Stith Thompson's summer Folklore Institute in Bloomington, Indiana, around 1950 and received significant encouragement from Thompson and Thompson's student William Hugh Jansen, who taught Roberts at the University of Kentucky. Roberts was also the magic tale collector whose work was earliest recognized by the folklore academy: in 1974, the American Folklore Society's Memoirs Series published his *Sang Branch Settlers*, a groundbreaking collection and study of one mountain family's repertoire of tales and songs. Yet, even if he gained recognition before Randolph did, Roberts's honor came late in his career: *Sang Branch Settlers* was published twenty-five years after he had begun collecting.

According to Roberts's closest friends and associates, his deferred recognition was largely due to a denial of academic support that hampered his progress throughout his career. Roberts had begun his folktale work at Berea College, but his colleague Loyal Jones asserted that he was rejected at Berea for his devotion to a traditional oral culture that the college administration was striving mightily to transcend, forget, and supplant with a standardizing academic culture (Jones 1997). Roberts left Berea early in his career, and only at the end of his life did he find honor there; his more than thirty years of field recordings are housed among the special collections in Hutchins Library. Hundreds of Märchen recorded by Roberts make this the nation's largest collection of audio-recorded mountain Märchen. Many of the tales have never been published or even transcribed, and they still await a study that will do them justice.

4) *Although the academy scorned Richard Chase, his influence on North American Märchen studies has been greater than that of all other American collectors and scholars combined.* The esteem in which Randolph and Roberts ultimately came to be held has not obscured the fact that Richard Chase has dominated perceptions of the American folktale more than any other man. Since Chase continually promoted and advertised his own work, it is not surprising that his influence has been so broadly felt outside the academy. What is remarkable is the extent to which his mystique has penetrated the scholarship on American traditional narrative. Because Chase figures largely in the three essays to follow, it is important to devote a certain amount of attention to him here.

If Randolph and Roberts were outsiders to the academic establishment, at least they found substantial welcome in the places where they conducted fieldwork. Born outside the Ozarks, Randolph nevertheless lingered so long in the mountains and produced work so strongly reflective of the native culture that at the time of his death he was known as "Mr. Ozark" by insiders and outsiders alike. Leonard Roberts collected in the region of his birth and apparently had a ready rapport with many of his informants. Richard Chase, to the contrary, was at least as much an outsider to his storytelling informants as to the academic folklore community. Born in 1904 in Huntsville, Alabama, to a New England family, Chase first sought his fortune in private schooling in the South, attended Vanderbilt University, and then migrated to the northeast, where he was impressed by a nostalgic vision of Old World folk culture and its possible survival in the Appalachians. David Whisnant has explored Chase's early career as a student, entrepreneur, and impressario of folk culture who regularly attempted to impose his personal fantasies on alien communities:

At a tea at Harvard's Longfellow House he heard of "a school in Kentucky" (Pine Mountain) that sounded interesting. Hitchhiking there in 1924, he heard mountain children singing ballads (as Olive Dame Campbell had in 1907 and Cecil Sharp had a decade later), and was captivated. It was, as he recalled more than fifty years later, "something vital." Taking a job as a country schoolteacher in Alabama, he used one of Sharp's books to teach ballads to his students. A short while later, he learned his first morris dances . . . at a private school in Connecticut. . . .

Shortly after 1930, he . . . [was] able to attach himself to the White Top [Virginia folk] festival. Just prior to the 1939 festival . . . a Richmond newspaper reported that Chase was training Richmond dancers for White Top and quoted [folk culture entrepreneur John] Powell as saying that the "children trained by [Chase] will . . . show the audiences how the children of 'Merrie England' some 500 years ago danced and played on the village green." (Whisnant 1983:202)

Witnessing the performances mounted by Chase at White Top in 1936, ethnomusicologist Charles Seeger pronounced the dancing "a flop" and labeled the festival a labor of "pseudo-scholarship," "reactionary to the core." Chase continued to attempt to graft his fantasies of folk culture onto the White Top festival, making it the stage for sword dances and puppet plays that he imported from his studies elsewhere but passed off as demonstrations of indigenous culture (Whisnant 1983:207–09). To Chase, his own imaginative productions were at least as representative of Appalachian folk culture as anything created by members of the local communities, a conviction that he acted on in donating to the Library of Congress a recorded performance of a mummers play he wrote and that the Appalachian children enacted under his direction.

Given Richard Chase's demonstrated tendency to treat his informants as his personal ventriloquist's dummies, it is difficult to imagine how folklorists with access to these well-established facts could have accepted so docilely Chase's representations of the American Märchen. Yet the extent to which Richard Chase's vision of the American magic tale has governed subsequent perception of the genre is difficult to overestimate.

Chase's effect on his popular audience is relatively easy to account for, as he stepped into a scholarly vacuum. In 1943, when *The Jack Tales* appeared, the recent Depression had fired an interest in grassroots culture and the subsequent war was cultivating nationalist fervor. Depression-era authors, most notably those working with the Federal Writers Project, had exploited the oral traditions of the tall tale and the joke. Yet Chase was the only writer on the scene who attempted to Americanize the oral genre most pervasively associated with both nationalism and escape: the magic tale. In the 1930s and 1940s, academic folklorist Joseph Médard Carrière (1937), WPA Federal Writers Project author Bright Lynn ([1938–39] 1987),[7] and others had assembled texts of European-American Märchen. These anthologies, collected from speakers of French and Spanish, emphasized the Old World nature of the tales, rather than the immediate New World environments from and to which the tellers so effectively spoke. As most Americans knew Märchen principally through the Grimms and the Hollywood translations of Walt Disney (the animated *Snow White* had become a nationwide hit in 1938), it is perhaps understandable that the British- and Irish-American forms of the genre would be seen as neither fully American nor fully "folk."

Chase, however, for all his preoccupations with ancient British tradition, presented his tales as a thoroughly American folk cultural self-celebration, perhaps one reason why they were received without the skepticism that attended his productions of sword dances and puppet plays. In his preface to *The Jack Tales*, Chase repeatedly stresses his conviction that their protagonist embodied aspects of an American character, distinct from his British forebears, and makes efforts to distinguish American Jack and his tales from readers' preconceptions concerning the Old World nature of the Märchen. Chase writes that Jack tales were told by the old to the young for the purpose of "keeping kids on the job" as they worked on such communal chores as canning. "This use of the tales," he concludes,

> seems to be a common custom in that neighborhood where everyone knows about "Jack" and where many. . . like to try their hand at telling about that boy's scrapes and adventures. It is through this natural oral process that our Appalachian giant-killer has acquired the easy-going, unpretentious rural American manners that make him so different from his English cousin, the cocksure, dashing young hero of the "fairy tale." (1943:ix)

According to Chase, then, Jack has a distinct personality, and it is that personality that signals the American-ness and uniqueness of the tales. He writes,

[I]t is always through the "little feller" *Jack* that we participate in the dreams, desires, ambitions of a whole people. . . .
Folk prosody has rarely presented so well-rounded a figure as *Jack*. *Reynard* is a one-sided rogue, the heroes of European collections of tales are many; other central characters are either supermen or gods. *Br'er Rabbit* seems to be the only one who shows many facets of character in a connected series of stories. *Jack,* however, is thoroughly human, the unassuming representative of a very large part of the American people. (xi–xii)

The reviewers and the public, together with that part of the academic folklore establishment that responded at all, enthusiastically bought Chase's construct. Picking up on the American theme laid out in the introduction, *Booklist* applauded the "humor, freshness, colorful American background, and the use of one character as a central figure in the cycle." In pronouncing *The Jack Tales* "meat for the student of folklore as well as for the lover of tall tales," *The Horn Book* helped Americanize the book by connecting it to the narrative genre most strongly associated with American folk culture (Chase 1993: [210]). Joseph Médard Carrière extended the refrain in a lengthy review, the first and longest to appear in the winter 1946 issue of the *Journal of American Folklore:* Chase's "Jack Tales reflect the true spirit of American folklore as it exists in the Southern Appalachians" (1946:76).

Chase was forthright in describing at least some of his methods, freely admitting to having created composite texts based on two or more performances. "We have taken the best of many tellings and correlated the best of all material into one complete version" (1943:xi), he writes, describing a methodology through which he assumed superiority to and control over his various sources. Yet there is further evidence that Chase was doing something other than constructing "ideal texts" closely modeled on the various performances that he had heard. The studies of Charles L. Perdue Jr. (1987) have identified changes greater and more intrusive than those Chase admitted, and Perdue's conclusions find crucial support from the family to whom Chase had attributed most of his Jack tales. In an interview with Ray Hicks, journalist Jo Woestendiek reported, "Hicks thinks the author took too many liberties, changing the stories and piecing them together so that they were different from the original tales" (1990:A12).

Richard Chase (1904–1988), as pictured in a brochure he
sent to Charles L. Perdue Jr. ca. 1980. *Courtesy Charles L.
Perdue Jr.*

As the popularity of the Jack tales grew, fed largely by Chase's tire-
less self-promotion, Chase himself took a contradictory stand toward
them: on the one hand, as announced in his Introduction, these tales
were particularly American and thus belonged to the entire country;
on the other hand, they were his and only his. Curiously, he never
seems to have asserted what folklorists now regard as obvious: that these
tales belonged most especially to the community of tellers among which
he found them. As Chase copyrighted the tales and discouraged others from telling them, he seems to have regarded himself as a one-man
national tradition, a Whitmanesque presence, containing multitudes.

Chase's treatment of the tales ran parallel to his treatment of their tellers. Folklorist Joe Wilson grew up six miles from Beech Creek and has an insider's perspective on Richard Chase's relations with the storytellers and others. He says,

> While Chase's editing, rewriting, performance, and copyrighting of sto-
> ries from tradition while claiming authenticity raises some serious ethi-
> cal issues for a folklorist, his extraordinary difficulties in that commu-
> nity were a result of personal activities. The community is hospitable
> and open-hearted, but Chase's repeated abusive treatment of his neigh-
> bors, particularly the children, angered the people of Beech Mountain.
> A community warning was delivered, and when it was ignored his house
> was burned and he was driven from the community. (Wilson, personal
> correspondence, 5 Sept. 2000)[8]

In my own research on Richard Chase, I find it difficult to make a cut-and-dried distinction between Chase the storyteller and Chase the neighbor, as both men treated their subjects with similar disre-spect. The ugly relationship that developed between Chase and the community that treated him generously, perhaps more than any other fact, should lead folklorists to question why Chase's work has taken the central position in American Märchen studies.

Strangely, the American folklore community has bought some of Chase's misrepresentations more enthusiastically than he himself pro-moted them. Although Chase subtitled the book to indicate a family tradition shared by "the descendants of Council Harmon," his notes clearly indicate that he drew upon the tales of twenty different narrators, only six of whom lived in the Beech Mountain area, the majority of whom were from Virginia, and at least eleven of whom were not related to the Harmon-Hicks family. Apparently reading his title more closely than his notes, folklorists to the present day tend to treat the Jack tales as an isolated, one-family tradition limited to Beech Mountain.[9]

Similarly, in spite of the fact that even Chase pointed out that the Jack tales were found extensively throughout the mountains, subse-quent collectors continued to rely primarily on Chase's Beech Moun-tain informants: among some thirty British- and Irish-American Märchen deposited by folklorists in the Library of Congress, all but six are from the Hicks-Harmon family. Of these, only the tales closest to Chase's in style and content have been released in recorded form.[10] Perhaps most puzzling, the only member of the family not recorded by

Chase has received no attention. Samuel Harmon of Maryville, Tennessee, died before Chase had a chance to collect from him. He was, significantly, also the only family member whose tales were sound-recorded before Chase compiled his book. In spite of the fact that Chase's book calls attention to Sam Harmon and his repertoire, the tale told by Harmon in this volume is the first to be published in any form.

5) *When American scholars belatedly recognized the Märchen as a form worthy of folklorists' study, they focused their attention on Old World traditions to the near exclusion of the British- and Irish-American tales.* As Randolph worked on, vigorously and alone with his collecting, and before Leonard Roberts began his, the formal study of folk narrative finally found a respected place in American folklore studies. This breakthrough was largely due to Stith Thompson, who created a major folklore industry at Indiana University. Though a British American himself, Thompson never specialized in British- or Irish-American narrative. Nor was he a field collector. His consuming interest was in identifying and classifying the thousands of Märchen and other narratives already published or housed in archives worldwide, and his current international reputation rests on his revisions of the international narrative catalog, *The Types of the Folktale* (Aarne and Thompson 1928, 1961), as well as upon his creation and then revision of the six-volume *Motif-Index of Folk-Literature* (1932–1937, 1955–58). Secondarily, Thompson performed tale type studies modeled on the European historic-geographic school, in which all available variants of a general plot were examined in an attempt to determine the story pattern's age and origin.

In the 1940s, Thompson began to transform Indiana University into the North American center for folk narrative study. In addition to his personal teaching and research, he began in 1941 to host a series of Summer Institutes at Indiana in which scholars from around the world gathered to exchange findings and ideas. Interestingly, all three of the major collectors of British- and Irish-American Märchen eventually attended one or more of these summer convocations, in telling ways: Vance Randolph, first in 1958, at age 66, after he had completed the manuscript of his final Märchen collection. Randolph remarked: "They wanted me there to look at—like Geronimo at the county fairs" (Cochran 1985:201). Leonard Roberts participated around 1950, as he was embarking upon his fieldwork. Richard Chase attended a summer institute in 1946—not as a scholar, but as an entertainer who directed "picnics and songfests and folk dances" (Thompson 1996:197).

As Thompson's training and influence began to make their marks on his American students, his international training emerged in their work. Warren E. Roberts, for example, produced a historic-geographic study of *The Kind and Unkind Girls* (1958) and worked with Thompson on *Types of Indic Oral Tales* (1960). Roberts went on to become a major figure in American folklore, but in his subsequent work he never revisited the Märchen studies. Other students, notably William Hugh Jansen, published substantial studies of American oral narrative, but in Jansen's case as in almost all the others, it was the humorous and nonfiction forms, the tall tale and the legend, into which he channeled his interests and expertise.

There were two major exceptions to this trend. Under Thompson's tutelage, Ernest W. Baughman published a comparative index, *Type and Motif-Index of the Folktales of England and North America* (1966). Baughman carefully curried every printed collection he could find, and, amazingly, discovered well over 300 published variants of North American Märchen (1966:ix). Mixing humility with wryness in a statement worthy of his teacher, Baughman declared: "The representation of the Märchen, while not impressive in comparison with other categories, indicates that there is perhaps a livelier interest in them than has been generally supposed" (xvi). Even as his work went to print, Baughman knew that it was obsolete: by including no texts published after 1959, it suffered from the fact that "most of the collections of Märchen have appeared in the last thirty years" (xvi). Now badly out of date, Baughman's index nonetheless remains an important research tool and provides more evidence than anyone should need that American folklorists unjustly ignored the Märchen.

The second Thompson student to persist in North American Märchen study was Herbert Halpert, who was to become the indisputable all-time expert in the field. Halpert's career substantially overlapped those of both Vance Randolph and Richard Chase. Randolph was to call Halpert "my only real friend among the folklorists" (Cochran 1985:203). Although they did not meet until 1956, the two men corresponded as early as 1939, long before Randolph published his first Märchen texts (173). By 1948 Halpert had begun his lonely

quest to find academic recognition for Randolph, maneuvering un-
successfully to have Randolph named vice president of the American
Folklore Society (191). The mutually admiring correspondence of
the two men grew into a partnership as Halpert annotated the first of
Randolph's Märchen-rich collections. When *Who Blowed Up the Church
House?* appeared, Halpert praised it as the "first major collection of
American-English white folktales for an adult audience" (Cochran
1985:198). The close association of Randolph and Halpert continued for four decades, ending only with Randolph's death in 1980.[11]

In a less congenial association, Halpert also worked with Richard
Chase, though indirectly. In preparing *The Jack Tales* for publication,
Chase sought the advice of Stith Thompson, who in turn urged his
student Halpert to provide annotations for the book. When Halpert
first took on the task, he did not realize the extent to which Chase
was changing his sources to create a children's book: "The fact that I
supplied scholarly references gave his first book a misleading respect-
ability that I regretted soon after I learned more about Chase's attitude towards tales" (letter to Carl Lindahl, February 21, 1991). Halpert
added weight to *The Jack Tales,* providing a concise history of the scholarly neglect of British- and Irish-American Märchen and then pro-
ceeding with annotations of the individual tales. The dual presence
of Chase's and Halpert's voices in *The Jack Tales* intensifies the ironic
status of that book, which represents both the worst and the best that
students of American Märchen could produce in 1943. Halpert's contributions as an annotator represent the finest published work done
on the North American Märchen before the 1990s, when his equally
impressive achievements as a collector finally began to be felt by folklorists—a topic I will visit at the end of this essay.

6) The final irony of the story is this: *even as evidence of a living
Märchen tradition mounted, it was, once again, the nonacademic popularizers who took the initiative and dominated the field.* In the 1970s, while
American Märchen studies continued to suffer neglect, the United
States experienced its greatest surge of popular interest in
storytelling since the end of World War II. Fed by schoolroom and
library storytelling sessions of the type that Chase pioneered and
continued to perform, the storytelling revival found a capital city in
1973 with the establishment of the National Storytelling Festival in
Jonesborough, Tennessee—in the heart of the Märchen country of

the southern Appalachians. The festival drew upon a core audience from organized storytelling guilds, some of which had been active since early in the century, but also sought and obtained the interest of a broad-based popular audience. To populate their stages, organizers drew upon professional storytellers, most of whom had little experience or knowledge of traditional oral storytelling, but the festival also capitalized on the localized oral traditions of the southern Appalachians by bringing in such traditional oral artists as Ray Hicks and his cousin Stanley.

Not surprisingly, Richard Chase sought recognition as the founder and grand old man of the new storytelling movement, but in one of the healthiest ironies of this curious history, the festival organizers and the professional storytelling community at large instead chose Ray Hicks as their icon. His grandfather and great uncle, Ben and Roby Hicks, had served as major sources for *The Jack Tales*. With Ray Hicks in the limelight, the Hicks-Harmon family effected a sweet revenge on Chase and finally began to emerge from his shadow.[12]

This unexpectedly pleasant shock should serve to awaken us: like the man who had no story, we've had a story all along, and it is time to take steps so that the story does not end as dismally as it has so far progressed.

Coda

This introduction cannot conclude without a discussion of the state of Märchen studies over the past few decades, an indication of some of the problems that persist and recent efforts to overcome them, and an articulation of the role of this volume in the process of recovering American Märchen and advancing their study.

The Storyteller's Journey, Joseph Sobol's history of the storytelling revival (1999), presents the narrative revival movement of recent decades as similar in nature to the folksong revival of the 1950s and 1960s. But for folklorists the differences are at least as persuasive as the similarities. The folklorist participants in the folksong revival did indeed draw upon and transform the folk artistry of various American singers, but in their roles as professional scholars they also copiously recorded, collected, and studied the work of the great traditional artists who inspired them and with whom they worked. In the 1960s, '70s, and

'80s, the leadership of the American Folklore Society was dominated by former folksong revival performers who had devoted their academic careers largely to the careful study of cultures of the performers they had once emulated. During this period, Roger D. Abrahams, Peggy Bulger, Kenneth J. Goldstein, Bess Lomax Hawes, Joseph Hickerson, Alan Jabbour, Charles and Nancy Martin Perdue, Ralph Rinzler, Ellen Steckert, and Barre Toelken—all former folk revival performers—attained prominence. Of these eleven, five have served as president of the Society. In contrast, no storytelling revival performer has achieved a similar role of leadership in the professional folklore community. It would be difficult to contest the allegation that a double standard has governed folklore circles, in which revivalist music is honored and revivalist storytelling shunned.

For its part, the storytelling movement has devoted far more energy to self-study than to the oral traditions upon which it rather indirectly draws. The major history of the revivalist movement is an auto-ethnography that examines the creation of festivals and the goals, motives, and styles of professional storytellers, but devotes only passing attention to traditional storytelling (Sobel 1999). To date, few of the published revivalist storytellers devote serious attention to the dynamics of narration in the traditional communities from which they take their tales.[13]

There is no good reason for folk narrative scholars and revival storytellers to persist in their mutual estrangement. The best evidence for my assertion is found in Edinburgh's School of Scottish Studies, at which, in recent decades, folklorists, traditional storytellers, and storytelling revivalists have worked together harmoniously and fruitfully. Among the school's faculty, the late Alan J. Bruford and the late Donald Archie MacDonald not only pursued the rigorous study of folk narrative, but also edited a major journal with both high scholarly standards and broad popular appeal, *Tocher*, through which they sought to share the tales collected by the school. The school's insistence that the tales belong to the people who told them and yet should be shared by all interested in them inspired scholars to become storytellers and storytellers to become scholars. Some of the finest student collectors, including Sheila Douglas and Barbara McDermitt, earned doctorates in part through their contributions to narrative study—but they also practice the art of storytelling.[14]

The North American situation is far different, but there are a few hopeful signs of change. In spite of the mutually exclusive positions taken by academic folklorists on the one hand and storytelling revivalists on the other, one scholarly work has sought the common ground between them. The single book that closely considers the relationship between traditional Märchen-telling and revivalist performances is *Jack in Two Worlds* (1994), edited by William Bernard McCarthy, which is also the only edited volume of essays devoted exclusively to American Märchen. As the book's title suggests, Richard Chase's influence persists in the focus on the Jack character, whose tales are examined to the exclusion of the substantial American Märchen traditions featuring female characters, or for that matter any of the many male protagonists who do not happen to be named Jack. *Jack in Two Worlds* devotes itself primarily to the transformative process through which traditional storytellers who learned their art at home later adapt their tales for public venues. Studies of Hicks-Harmon family storytellers Frank Proffitt Jr. and Maud Long, as well as of Jack tale tellers from other families, explore the tellers' memories of how their stories were once shared, discuss ways in which recent performances were adapted for more public venues, and present performances from each featured storyteller. The book devotes about half of its length to the Hicks-Harmon family, but refreshingly expands the inquiry to treat other previously unstudied performers and their performances.

Jack in Two Worlds belongs to the growing literature on the transformation of private traditions into more public ones. However, like David Whisnant's masterpiece, *All That Is Native and Fine* (1983), *Jack* deals in great detail with the process and end products of transformation without giving sufficient consideration to the root traditions so dramatically transformed. I believe the work of folklorists must include drawing as close as possible to the practice of private traditions on their own terms; the contributions of *Jack in Two Worlds* would be enhanced by further exploration of the informal and domestic traditions that form the basis for recent public performances. The present volume is thus primarily an exercise in "recovery" scholarship, applying old tools in new ways to deepen our knowledge of traditional storytelling practices, styles, and contexts that have been long ignored.

In the past thirteen years, two major books, each combining both texts and extensively researched interpretations, have helped to establish the breadth and nature of British- and Irish-American Märchen-telling. The articles in this issue further develop these approaches. Given the scant attention previously paid to Märchen traditions, it is essential that much of this work be reconstructive, addressing texts collected from long-dead tellers. The masterpiece of reconstruction in the study of North American Märchen is Charles L. Perdue Jr.'s *Outwitting the Devil: Jack Tales from Wise County Virginia* (1987). It publishes for the first time twenty-eight manuscript tales that James Taylor Adams collected in the early 1940s from family members and neighbors in mountains of western Virginia. Richard Chase drew upon these same texts to create *The Jack Tales*, and they, together with Perdue's careful comparative readings, demonstrate precisely how Chase altered some of the tales that appeared in his book. Perdue's work should have released us from several of the dominating preconceptions concerning the Jack tales, most notably the idea that they belonged primarily to one extended North Carolina family. The extent of Perdue's contribution has not yet been digested by most folklorists.[15]

In "Is Old Jack Really Richard Chase?" (this volume) Perdue extends his work to consider the changes that Chase made in successive printings of the "same" tale. In the absence of living witnesses, this examination not only provides ample evidence of Chase's extremely loose methods, but also poses interesting questions concerning the nature and origins of Chase's notions of style. In a second set of textual comparisons, Perdue weighs certain traits of Chase's tales against those collected earlier by others in the same region. As all of these narrators are now dead, Perdue's close reading of the surviving textual record performs a vital service in alerting us to those details that Chase most probably added to and excised from the oral performances in order to shape his own aesthetic.

Most vital to recovering North American Märchen is finding and listening to their living performers. For more than sixty years, the folklore academy's best listener was Herbert Halpert, whose work as an annotator of Randolph's and Chase's tales has already been discussed. Beyond his bibliographical work, Halpert spent three decades collecting North American Märchen. In 1939, he collected tales from Samuel Harmon; these comprise the earliest recordings of mountain Märchen to be found in the collections of the Archive of Folk Culture. Through the 1940s, Halpert collected numerous narratives in the New Jersey Pines, and in the 1960s, with his colleague J. D. A. Widdowson, he embarked upon a massive project to collect, transcribe, study, and publish the Märchen of Newfoundland.

After more than thirty years, *Folktales of Newfoundland* (1996) reached print, in two volumes of nearly 1300 pages and more than 150 folktale texts, providing copious evidence of the extent and the "resilience" (in the co-editors' words) of North American Märchen traditions. Combining Halpert's unsurpassed skills as both collector and annotator, this enormous contribution also presents, in its comparative notes, a virtual library of information on the British- and Irish-derived magic tale traditions of all of North America. The comparative notes and bibliographies expand considerably on Baughman's earlier work, especially in providing long-published Canadian parallels that Baughman and most other scholars trained in the United States had missed.

Joining Halpert and Widdowson in the preparation of *Folktales of Newfoundland* was Martin Lovelace, who provided the motifs and motif index for the entire collection and whose knowledge of its contents is equaled only by that of his co-editors. In his essay on "Jack and His Masters" (this volume), Lovelace presents the first critical study based on the narratives assembled in *Folktales of Newfoundland*. Examining various ways in which the male protagonists face situations of subservience and work, Lovelace contributes to the study of North American Märchen in a number of ways. First, by describing in great detail a maritime Canadian Jack, Lovelace implies a strong caution against reading North American Jack tales exclusively in terms of the southern Appalachian context. Second, in tying his analysis of the tales closely to the working conditions of the narrators, Lovelace introduces ways of reading the tales in light of the economic and social dimensions of the storytelling communities.

Third, to a much greater extent than the other essays in this volume, Lovelace draws upon recent European Märchen studies to inform his interpretations. When Stith Thompson retired from his Indiana University professorship in 1959, the historic-geographic school was still devoting its energies to the patterns, rather than the meanings, contexts, and functions, of Märchen. Since that time, numerous studies—most notably Bengt Holbek's exhaustive analysis of

Danish Märchen (1987) and the North American John Minton's careful reading of one African-American tale type (1993)—have redirected the focus of comparative textual study toward the exploration of social meanings projected and carried in the tale. All three of the following essays present comparative studies informed to some extent by the historic-geographic method of reading traits, patterns, and motifs, but all also direct these formal exercises toward the search for specifically socially-situated values and meanings, not toward the contemplation of form for form's sake.

Although American folklore studies have largely abandoned such multi-textual comparisons, much as they have abandoned the Märchen, these three essays, I hope, will serve as a useful corrective. The excesses of the performance school have sometimes led analysts to focus so myopically on the details of a single, contemporary narration that they have lost perspective on the values, meanings, and aesthetics shared by the communities in which the tales normally unfold, in much different circumstances, when the collector is not present. As Barbara McDermitt has observed, many of the recent analyses of Jack tales are based disproportionately on uncharacteristic performances in which only the narrator and collector are present (1986:29–30). Such contexts typically give rise to what I call "conspiratorial interpretations," narratives and readings based far more firmly on the transient relationship of one narrator and one collector than on the community values, aesthetic expectations, performance styles, and contexts that typically inspire and shape the tales (Lindahl 1997:54–56). The most important obligation of the folklorist, I believe, is to discover and explore these latter concerns.

By 1997 the formidable publications of Halpert, Widdowson, Lovelace, and Perdue had all appeared. Seeking a forum in which their contributions could be examined and built upon, I obtained funding from a variety of sources to host a conference on "American Magic: The Fates of Oral Fiction in the New World," which took place at the University of Houston in October 1997. The essays by Perdue and Lovelace presented here are developments of the papers that they presented at that symposium.

My contribution, "Sounding a Shy Tradition," was not presented at the conference, as it was precluded by my role as host. But Linda Dégh, my teacher and mentor in Märchen studies, did present a vital consideration of "The Artist at the Center," a plea for renewed and deeper examinations of the great storytellers upon whose craft traditional Märchen-telling most depends. My essay applies Dégh's precepts to American narrators. In it, I examine certain claims about Märchen artistry advanced by those who study it more as a literary than as an oral form, and I then consider written representations of oral Märchen in the published collections of Chase, Roberts, and Randolph. Most importantly, I attempt to weigh this written work against the brilliant oral performances of Samuel Harmon (as recorded by Halpert in 1939) and Jane Muncy (as recorded by Roberts in 1949 and 1955, and by me in 2000). My study is guided by the conviction that the recent reconstructions, collections, and annotations, which have added so much to our knowledge, must be supplemented by lengthy learning sessions in which storytellers not only demonstrate their art, but also communicate their ideas about the tales' meanings, and in which the listeners who have long heard and admired such performances demonstrate and discuss their reactions to the tales. In searching out the storytellers and their traditional audiences, I was not able to find any surviving members of Samuel Harmon's storytelling community; however, in 1997 I interviewed and learned from four members of Jane Muncy's family Märchen circle, and in 2000 I finally reached her and spent a few days with her and six family members who had long enjoyed her tales. Jane and her aunt Glen not only performed impressively, but all also spoke eloquently and at great length about their family traditions.

After submitting our essays for publication, Perdue, Lovelace, and I were invited to supplement our writings with folktale texts. We have seized this opportunity to feature prominently the ultimate source of and inspiration for our work.[16] Beyond the pleasure that we believe readers will derive from them, these tales are presented with at least four specific purposes in mind.

First, three texts document the differences between Richard Chase's published tales and the traditions that he tapped. Charles L. Perdue Jr. contributes two written reconstructions—one by Chase and one by James Taylor Adams—of the same performance: Polly Johnson's telling of "Jack and the Bull." Similarly, I present the first published transcription of Samuel Harmon's "Stiff Dick,"

Dicy Adams (1893–1983) of Big Laurel, Virginia, contributed
several tales to the collections of her husband, James Taylor
Adams, in the early 1940s. This photo was taken in 1980;
according to her great-grandson Fletcher Dean, she "still loved
to tell tales." *Courtesy Fletcher Dean*

a cognate of "Jack and the Varmints" as retold by Richard Chase in
The Jack Tales (1943:58–66). By examining Harmon's oral performance in tandem with Chase's widely available published version
(as I do in "Sounding a Shy Tradition"), readers will discover substantial stylistic differences between the two. Second, to demonstrate the variety of narrative style within a single family, I present
two different, recent performances of "Rawhead and Bloodybones"
by two narrators who first and most often heard the tale from the
same teller. Third, to suggest the depth, variety, quality, and extent of long-available Märchen texts that nevertheless remained
unpublished and unstudied at the end of the twentieth century,

Charles Perdue submits "Jack and the Green Man," written down in 1945, to which I add Samuel Harmon's earlier-cited 1939 performance of "Stiff Dick." Fourth, in Alice Lannon's "The Ship That Sailed on Land and Water" and Jane Muncy's "Merrywise" and "Rawhead and Bloodybones," all recorded within the past two years, Martin Lovelace and I hint at the extent and quality of contemporary Märchen-telling as practiced by exceptional traditional narrators in North America today.

Each of the essays and tales adds something to the understanding of American Märchen; it is my hope that, taken together, they will offer much more than the sum of their parts by calling attention to recent, but neglected, developments and by suggesting approaches as yet untried.

In hopes that these contributions will meet their standards, I end by recognizing the three scholars whose work has most informed this issue: Linda Dégh, whose knowledge of Märchen-telling as a living art is unequaled; Chuck Perdue, on the occasion of his seventieth birthday, and in appreciation of the extraordinary rigor and integrity with which he has fought to represent folk communities on their own terms; and Herbert Halpert, who for sixty years did more than the rest of the scholarly community combined to advance the study of North American Märchen. Professor Halpert died, at age eighty-nine, on December 29, 2000, as this volume was in production. I hope that my introduction has conveyed some measure of the importance of his work, and some idea of how much he will be missed. This volume is dedicated to his memory.

University of Houston
Texas

Acknowledgments

The three papers and introduction that compose this volume were all either presented at or largely inspired by the conference "American Magic: The Fates of Oral Fiction in the New World," which took place at the University of Houston in October 1997. I would like to thank various colleagues and organizations for attending, funding, and supporting this conference. A residential fellowship from the Virginia Foundation for the Humanities in the spring of 1997 afforded me the time and research opportunity to plan the conference and focus its framing issues. The eight invited conferees—Barry Jean Ancelet, the late Daniel J. Crowley, Linda Dégh, Martin Lovelace, W. K. McNeil, John Minton, Juha Pentikäinen, and Charles L. Perdue Jr.—taught me much. The Counsel General of Canada and the University of Houston's American Cultures Program, Department of English, Honors College, and Women's Studies Program provided funding. I would like to thank Dorothy Baker, Harmon Boertien, Lynn Dale, Elizabeth Gregory, Crystal Jackson, DeLinda Marzette, Michelle Miller, Bill Monroe, and Lee Winniford for their personal contributions to its success.

Notes

1. The plot outlined here most closely summarizes the Scottish Gaelic performance of Angus MacLellan (1997:201–02). Identified as type 2412B in *Types of the Irish Folktale* (O'Sullivan and Chistiansen 1963), the story is well known in the traditions of Ireland (Danaher 1998:12–14; Glassie 1982:319–23; O'Sullivan 1964:182–84) and Scotland (Douglas 1987:67–69). Editors often choose it to begin or to close their anthologies. As a story about the importance of stories, this tale, not surprisingly, has become a master narrative of the storytelling revival, one of whose members labels it a "totemic" tale (Sobel 1999:41).

2. There is no consistently applied label for the tales discussed here. In German, *Märchen* may signify many types of oral fiction, but English-speaking folklorists tend to use the term as a substitute for the German *Zaubermärchen*, or "magic tale," the oral equivalent of the written "fairy tale." In my introduction and essay here, I apply "Märchen" a bit more broadly than some folklorists, to indicate not only the wonder-laden stories that Aarne and Thompson (1961) label "Tales of Magic" (AT 300–749) but also many of the tales that they classify as "Religious Tales" (AT 750–849), "Novelle" (AT 850–999), "Tales of the Stupid Ogre" (AT 1000–1199), and "Jokes and Anecdotes" (AT 1200–). My working definition for Märchen is "a multi-episodic fictional narrative told for entertainment and, though often humorous in effect, not primarily humorous in intent."

Some writers use the term "Jack tales" exclusively to identify the North Carolina-based narrative tradition of the Hicks-Harmon family, whose earliest recorded name for this corpus was "Old Jack, Will, and Tom Tales" (Carter 1925:340). Whether or not "Jack tales" was a term in extensive circulation before Richard Chase used it to title his influential book (Chase 1943), many Appalachian narrators from diverse family traditions now identify their stories with this term, and among some families it is a general tag for any Märchen, whether or not it includes a character named Jack. In his essay, Charles L. Perdue Jr. focuses on the two localized traditions that Chase tapped—the Hicks-Harmon family narratives and tales collected by James Taylor Adams in Wise County, Virginia—and necessarily applies the term much as Chase did. Because my essay covers diverse traditions from Kentucky, Tennessee, and the Ozarks in addition to the Hicks-Harmon and Wise County tales, I apply the term "mountain

Märchen" generally to Appalachian and Ozark traditions and use "British- and Irish-American Märchen" for the entire North American corpus, including the Newfoundland narratives examined by Martin Lovelace in his essay.

3. Examples of this tendency to summarize (often while offering ongoing interpretations in the course of narration) can be seen in Glen Muncy Anderson's "Rawhead and Bloodybones" and Jane Muncy Fugate's "Merrywise," both included in this volume. Mrs. Anderson insisted repeatedly that she was not a storyteller, and thus it is not surprising that she chose to relate her tale more as a summary cum commentary than as a performance. In contrast, Jane Muncy Fugate is recognized as a master narrator by her family, but she also begins her story with a commentary on the characters before fully engaging the tale as a performance rather than as a report.

4. The Farmer-Muncy family examined in "Sounding a Shy Tradition" presents one example of a tale-rich family that did not have an extensive singing tradition. I am aware of other Kentucky families that have similarly nurtured tales to the exclusion of musical traditions.

5. The one exception is Gardner (1937). For a fuller discussion of the major British- and Irish-American Märchen collections, see note 1 of "Sounding a Shy Tradition."

6. This chronology of Randolph's folklore writings is based on the thorough bibliographic research of Cochran and Luster (1979).

7. Lynn collected magic tales from Guadalupe Baca de Gallegos during 1938–1939, while working for the New Mexico Federal Writers' Project, but they were not published until 1987.

8. Wilson's observations were included in e-mail correspondence to me on September 5, 2000; they were corroborated by W. K. McNeil in a telephone interview on August 13, 2000.

9. See, for example, the earlier discussion of Michael Ann Williams, as well as note 15, below.

10. Ellis 1994:101; see note 3 from "Sounding a Shy Tradition."

11. Halpert described the genesis of their friendship: "I had long admired Randolph's first two books on the Ozarks as one of the few discussions of the folklife of a region, and also had a high regard for both the scope and the annotation of his enormous folksong collection. I was disappointed that his excellent tall tale book had no comparative notes and wrote to him to say so. That's how we got to work together" (personal communication, February 25, 1991).

12. Sobol (1999:105–16) provides a brief account of Hicks's rise to fame and "canonization" at the Jonesborough festival and alludes briefly to Chase's attempt to gain similar recognition. Sobol also cites the important role folklorist Tom Burton of Eastern Tennessee State University played in advising festival directors to bring Ray to the festival, one of the major exceptions to the general rule of the folklore academy's neglect of mountain Märchen-telling traditions.

13. One notable exception to this rule is storyteller Diane Wolkstein's collection of Haitian tales (1980). This work clearly projects her aesthetics of and passion for storytelling, but it also describes in significant detail the Haitian performances that provided her with source narratives. By gracefully juxtaposing careful, respectful observations with demonstrations of personal artistry,

Wolkstein's book could serve as a model for revivalists who wish to do justice both to their sources and to their craft.

14. Barbara McDermitt (1999) provides a brief and illuminating assessment of the traditional, academic, and revivalist storytelling traditions in Scotland.

15. Appearing eleven years after Perdue's work, Ted Olson's otherwise excellent treatment of Chase and the Hicks-Harmon family perpetuates the idea of the Jack tales as an "uncommon local storytelling tradition," discussing only the involvement of the North Carolina Hicks-Harmon family and neglecting the fact—admitted by Chase himself and unquestionably re-affirmed by Perdue's study—that the majority of Chase's informants were not members of this family (Olson 1998:76–78).

16. The narratives included in this volume were transcribed by various individuals using slightly different systems. I produced the transcriptions of "Stiff Dick," "Merrywise," and the two versions of "Rawhead and Bloodybones." All four adhere to the principles set out in *Swapping Stories: Folktales from Louisiana* (Lindahl, Owens, and Harvison 1997:27–29):

> 1) I generally avoid dialect and colloquial spellings, employing them only when, in my judgment, the narrator seems to be using variant pronunciation for purposes of effect or characterization. For example, in her performance of "Merrywise," Jane Muncy changes her pronunciation toward the end of the tale, particularly when describing the witch and rendering the witch's speech: although Jane typically uses the standard "get," "them," and "running" elsewhere in her tale, she changes her pronunciation to say "git," "em," and "runnin" toward the end. In Samuel Harmon's "Stiff Dick" and in Glen Muncy Anderson's version of "Rawhead and Bloodybones," I sometimes render "em" instead of "them," because both narrators employ both the standard "them" and the colloquial "em" pronunciations, and it seems to me that "em" represents a sort of minor stylistic choice on the part of both narrators. My avoidance of dialect spellings is based on convictions best expressed in the work of Dennis Preston (1982; 1983). Preston offers strong evidence to support his contention that such spellings (which, he demonstrates, have been used disproportionately and inaccurately by folklorists in rendering the speech of African Americans and Southern whites) represent a condescending professional bias.
>
> 2) Nevertheless (again following Preston), I have tried to transcribe faithfully all morphological variations from Standard English. Thus, these transcriptions record the use of such common variations as "come" (past tense) instead of "came" and "ain't" instead of "isn't."
>
> 3) Ellipses are used exclusively to indicate that one or more of the speaker's words have been deleted from the transcription. I have transcribed every audible word in all four tales; only in two cases, where the speaker's words were unintelligible to me, have I used ellipses. However, in quoting information given by the narrators about their lives and art, and in quoting parts of the tales for purposes of analysis, I have often employed ellipses to excise words not directly relevant to the point under discussion.
>
> 4) Em-dashes indicate pauses and false starts, as well as grammatical shifts that present little problems in oral communication but may prove confusing to a reader without a marker to indicate that the narrator's syntax is changing course.

5) Italics indicate vocal emphasis; I have used these sparingly, and most often when the emphasized word seems to me to alter, rather than merely to intensify, the narrator's meaning.

Martin Lovelace transcribed Alice Lannon's telling of "The Ship that Sailed on Land and Water" using the system described by Herbert Halpert and J. D. A. Widdowson in *Folktales of Newfoundland: The Resilience of the Oral Tradition* (1996) and reproduced in note 3 of his essay here. The tales provided by Charles L. Perdue Jr. are copies of archival transcriptions.

References Cited

Aarne, Antti, and Stith Thompson
1928   *The Types of the Folktale: A Classification and Bibliography.* Revised ed. Folklore Fellows Communications No. 74. Helsinki: Suomalainen Tiedeakatemia.
1961   *The Types of the Folktale: A Classification and Bibliography.* 2d. revised ed. Folklore Fellows Communications No. 184. Helsinki: Suomalainen Tiedeakatemia.

Baughman, Ernest W.
1966   *Type and Motif-Index of the Folktales of England and North America.* Indiana University Folklore Studies No. 20. The Hague: Mouton.

Carrière, Joseph Médard
1937   *Tales from the French Folklore of Missouri.* Northwestern Studies in the Humanities No. 1. Evanston, Ill.
1946   Review of *The Jack Tales* by Richard Chase. *Journal of American Folklore* 59:74–77.

Carter, Isabel Gordon
1925   "Mountain White Folk-Lore: Tales from the Southern Blue Ridge." *Journal of American Folklore* 38:340–74.

Chase, Richard
1943   *The Jack Tales.* Boston: Houghton Mifflin.
1993   *The Jack Tales.* Fiftieth anniversary paperback edition. Boston: Houghton Mifflin.

Cochran, Robert
1985   *Vance Randolph: An Ozark Life.* Urbana and Chicago: University of Illinois Press.

Cochran, Robert, and Michael Luster
1979   *For Love and for Money: The Writings of Vance Randolph.* Arkansas College Folklore Archive Monograph Series No. 2. Batesville, Ark.: Riverside Graphics.

Danaher, Kevin
1998   *Folktales from the Irish Countryside.* Reprint, Cork and Dublin: Mercier Press.

Douglas, Sheila
1987   *"The King o the Black Art" and Other Folktales.* Aberdeen, Scotland: Aberdeen University Press.

Ellis, Bill
1994 "The Gentry-Long Tradition and Roots of Revivalism: Maud Gentry Long." In *Jack in Two Worlds: Contemporary North American Tales and Their Tellers*, ed. William Bernard McCarthy, 93–106. Chapel Hill: University of North Carolina Press.

Gardner, Emelyn Elizabeth
1937 *Folklore from the Schoharie Hills, New York*. Ann Arbor: University of Michigan Press.

Glassie, Henry
1982 *Passing the Time in Ballymenone: Culture and History of an Ulster Community*. Philadelphia: University of Pennsylvania Press. (Reprint, Bloomington: Indiana University Press, 1995.)
1985 *Irish Folk Tales*. New York: Pantheon.

Halpert, Herbert
1943 "Appendix and Parallels." In *The Jack Tales*, ed. Richard Chase, 183–200. Boston: Houghton Mifflin.

Halpert, Herbert, and J. D. A. Widdowson, eds.
1996 *Folktales of Newfoundland: The Resilience of the Oral Tradition*. With the assistance of Martin J. Lovelace and Eileen Collins. Music transcription and commentary by Julia C. Bishop. 2 vols. Publications of the American Folklore Society, New Series. Patrick B. Mullen, series editor. World Folktale Library, vol. 3. Carl Lindahl, series editor. New York: Garland.

Holbek, Bengt
1987 *Interpretation of Fairy Tales: Danish Folklore in a European Perspective*. Folklore Fellows Communications No. 239. Helsinki: Suomalainen Tiedeakatemia.

Jones, Loyal
1997 Interview conducted by Carl Lindahl, May 3.

Lindahl, Carl
1997 "The Power of Being Outnumbered." *Louisiana Folklore Miscellany* 12:43–75.

Lynn, Bright
1938–1939 Autobiography and magic tales collected from Guadalupe Baca de Gallegos, for the New Mexico Federal Writers' Project. Eventually Published in *Two Guadalupes: Legends and Magic Tales from Northern New Mexico*, ed. Marta Weigle, 33–125. Santa Fe: Ancient City Press, 1987.

MacLellan, Angus
1997 *Stories from South Uist*. Trans. John Lorne Campbell. Edinburgh: Birlinn.

McCarthy, William Bernard
1994 *Jack in Two Worlds: Contemporary North American Tales and Their Tellers*. Tales edited by William Bernard McCarthy, Cheryl Oxford, and Joseph Daniel Sobol. Chapel Hill and London: University of North Carolina Press.

McDermitt, Barbara Rice Damran
1986 "A Comparison of a Scottish and American Storyteller and Their Märchen Repertoires." Ph. D. dissertation, University of Edinburgh.

1999   "Storytelling Traditions in Scotland." In *Traditional Storytelling Today*, ed. Margaret Read MacDonald, 289–300. Chicago: Fitzroy Dearborn.

McNeil, W. K.

1999   "Where Have All the Märchen Gone? Or, Don't They Tell Those Little Stories Any More?" In *Traditional Storytelling Today*, ed. Margaret Read MacDonald, 387–93. Chicago: Fitzroy Dearborn.

Minton, John

1993   *"Big 'Fraid and Little 'Fraid": An Afro-American Folktale*. Folklore Fellows Communications No. 253. Helsinki: Suomalainen Tiedeakatemia.

Olson, Ted

1998   *Blue Ridge Folklife*. Jackson: University Press of Mississippi.

O'Sullivan, Sean

1964   *Folktales of Ireland*. Chicago and London: University of Chicago Press.

O'Sullivan, Sean, and Reider Th. Christiansen

1963   *The Types of the Irish Folktale*. Folklore Fellows Communications No. 188. Helsinki: Suomalainen Tiedeakatemia.

Perdue, Charles L., Jr.

1987   *Outwitting the Devil: Jack Tales from Wise County Virginia*. Santa Fe: Ancient City Press.

Randolph, Vance

1944   *Funny Stories about Hillbillies*. Girard, Kans.: Haldeman-Julius.

1951   "Bedtime Stories from Missouri." *Western Folklore* 10:1–10.

1952   *Who Blowed Up the Church House? and Other Ozark Folk Tales*. New York: Columbia University Press.

1955   *The Devil's Pretty Daughter and Other Ozark Folk Tales*. New York: Columbia University Press.

1957   *The Talking Turtle and Other Ozark Folk Tales*. New York: Columbia University Press.

1958   *Sticks in the Knapsack and Other Ozark Folk Tales*. New York: Columbia University Press.

1965   *Hot Springs and Hell, and Other Folk Jests and Anecdotes from the Ozarks*. Hatboro, Penn.: Folklore Associates.

Roberts, Leonard

1949–80 Leonard Roberts Collection. Hutchins Library, Berea College. Berea, Ky.

1955   *South from Hell-fer-Sartin: Kentucky Mountain Folktales*. Lexington: University Press of Kentucky.

1974   *Sang Branch Settlers*. Austin; reprint Pikeville, Ky: Pikeville College Press,1980.

Roberts, Warren E.

1958   *The Tale of the Kind and Unkind Girls*. Berlin: Walter de Gruyter.

Sobol, Joseph Daniel

1999   *The Storytellers' Journey: An American Revival*. Urbana and Chicago: University of Illinois Press.

Thompson, Stith

1932–1937 *Motif-Index of Folk-Literature: A Classification of Narrative Elements in Folktales, Ballads, Myths, Fables, Mediaeval Romances, Exempla, Fabliaux,*

Jest-Books and Local Legends. 6 vols. Folklore Fellows Communications Nos. 106–09, 116, 117. Helsinki: Suomalainen Tiedeakatemia.

1946   *The Folktale.* New York: Dryden Press.

1955–1958 *Motif-Index of Folk-Literature: A Classification of Narrative Elements in Folktales, Ballads, Myths, Fables, Mediaeval Romances, Exempla, Fabliaux, Jest-Books and Local Legends.* 2d. ed. 6 vols. Bloomington: Indiana University Press.

1996   *A Folklorist's Progress: Reflections of a Scholar's Life.* Ed. John H. McDowell, Inta Gale Carpenter, Donald Braid, and Erika Peterson-Veatch. Special Publications of the Folklore Institute No. 5. Indiana University, Bloomington.

Thompson, Stith, and Warren E. Roberts

1960   *Types of Indic Oral Tales: India, Pakistan, and Ceylon.* Folklore Fellows Communications No. 180. Helsinki: Suomalainen Tiedeakatemia.

Whisnant, David E.

1983   *All That Is Native and Fine: The Politics of Culture in an American Region.* Chapel Hill and London: University of North Carolina Press.

Williams, Michael Ann

1995   *Great Smoky Mountains Folklife.* Jackson: University Press of Mississippi.

Woestendiek, Jo

1990   Interview with Ray Hicks. *Winston Salem Journal,* July 22:A9, A12.

Wolkstein, Diane

1980   *The Magic Orange Tree and Other Haitian Folktales.* New York: Schocken Books.

Two Tellings of "Merrywise": 1949 and 2000

Among the major collectors of American Märchen, only Leonard Roberts extensively recorded tales from children. Of these young storytellers, none has received more praise than Jane Muncy, who has become known for five tales she told Roberts in 1949, when she was eleven years old, and for four more she told him in 1955; the first five appear in Roberts's *South from Hell-fer-Sartin* (1955) and the remaining four are published in his *Old Greasybeard: Tales from the Cumberland Gap* (1969). "Merrywise," Jane's favorite among these tales, appears in the earlier book.

On June 3, 2000, I recorded Jane—now married and named Jane Muncy Fugate. It had been fifty-one years since she had last recorded "Merrywise." The present performance, when read in tandem with Jane's first published version, offers remarkable evidence of both the tenacity and the dynamism of her family's oral artistry.

Jane Muncy Fugate's family storytelling tradition represents an important but little-studied dimension of the Appalachian Märchen. Scholars have devoted extensive attention to the Hicks-Harmon family, whose tales, recorded from more than a dozen family members over a span of eight decades, have retained a remarkable stability of plot. Muncy family narrators, in contrast, have treated the plots of their cherished tales very freely and have tended to rely instead on a few vivid images as the basis for reconstructing their tales in performance. Furthermore, the Muncys were a family of avid readers who not only retold the tales they had read in books, but also added literary flourishes to the tales they retained from oral tradition. My essay "Sounding a Shy Tradition" describes the Muncy family's oral artistry in greater detail.

Jane performed "Merrywise" for her husband Robert Fugate and me in Melbourne, Florida, on June 3, 2000. She learned the tale from her grandmother, Sidney Farmer Muncy, of Leslie County, Kentucky—a strong-willed, well-educated, former teacher who used folktales as one of many tools for educating Jane. Jane's father enlisted in the Marines at the outbreak of World War II and Jane was sent to live with her grandmother.

Jane recalled the process through which she came to hear and share her grandmother's stories:

> *First time that I remember meeting her, I was about four, and my father and mother had lived in Pennsylvania. World War II had just started—the bombing of Pearl Harbor—and my father and mother were getting a divorce. And my father won custody and he wrote her a telegram. I saw the telegram when I was*

just a child, and the telegram said, "MOM, COME AND GET JANE—I'M GOING IN / STOP"
—and so, that she did. She got on a train . . . all the way to Pennsylvania—
Philadelphia—to pick up little Jane. And, she was a stranger to me, and I was
basically a stranger to her. She was sixty-seven and, as far as she knew, I was
going to be her charge for a long time, because the war had started, my dad was
going in the Marines, and he was going to be far away, and she was going to
have me on her own.

And she, she did just that. She told me many times that I was her salvation,
that I kept her young. She slept with me. She cuddled me. She said I was terribly,
terribly thin and small, and that she must revive me. She was surprised that I
was living, as thin and small as I was, and she could carry me on one arm. . . .

. . . [O]ur life together alone took on a pattern of creativity on her part to
keep me occupied and quiet, . . . and [it] also [included] teaching: teaching me
how to read, teaching me how to listen to stories, and teaching me how to read the
censored letters that came from my father and my Uncle Gill. Uncle Gill was a
straightforward kind of guy, . . . and he would write on and on and on and
many times say things that were disclosing things the war effort people didn't
want him to disclose. So his letters would be one or two sentences, and then a
whole lot of cut-outs, and one or two sentences, and a whole lot of cut-outs—
which was very frustrating to us, as we were trying to figure out where he was,
because he couldn't tell us. My dad, however, was more cunning, and he would
say things to her like, "Mom, you know that necklace that I sent to Jane? Well,*
that necklace came from Uncle Sol's store. Remember Uncle Sol? You can remem-
ber him, where he lived out on that little place all by himself." And she would go*
get the map of Europe and the East, and she would say, "Ah, okay, it means he's*
on the Solomon Islands, it's an island all by itself, and that's the Sol he's talking
about, and they have shells." And so we, we had like a little war map and flags*
and his picture nearby. And he was my hero.

And she was my comfort. One of the things that she did for me for comfort
was, I was allowed to sleep with her. I think in the beginning it was because she
had a big bed, and not a little bed. But maybe not. I think families did sleep
together a great deal in those years.

But the, the comforting thing we did at night was, we looked at the map one
more time, we listened to the war news, we got into our nightgowns—I don't
remember what mine looked like, but I remember hers was white and cotton and
it had tiny bits of lace around the neck and around the sleeves. And then we
wound up the clock. If we lived in a place that had a fireplace, we banked the fire,
and we went to bed. But that wasn't the end of the day, because the end of the day
usually involved her telling me at least a couple of stories that she'd heard as a
child—and then drifting off to sleep. I would always drift off to sleep with my ear
at her back, because I liked to hear her heart beat. . . .

So we were bedtime buddies and bedtime storytellers, and I would tell her [of] a
favorite *story I wanted to hear, and she would usually tell that, and then she would*

tell me the favorite story she wanted to tell me, which I realize now as I'm older: they were not always folktales handed down from generation to generation, but sometimes found in fairytale books, sometimes found in the Arabian Nights stories. Sometimes they were stories about her family, things that actually happened in her family.

But it was a long tradition during that period—of about six years before I saw my father again. . . . So that's how we got to the storytelling phase of our lives. And it continued. Even after Daddy came home.

Jane's father was back in Kentucky in 1949 when Leonard Roberts recorded her first version of "Merrywise" and other tales in a schoolhouse in Hyden. Even Jane's earliest recordings reveal how well she had learned her grandmother's lessons; on the tapes, she emerges as a spirited, mature, artful, and self-assured narrator.

When Roberts recorded Jane again in 1955, she was seventeen, now performing with persuasive adult skills. Those were Jane's last recorded tales before I met her at her home in Melbourne, Florida, in June 2000. During the intervening forty-five years, she had been retelling her grandmother's and her aunts' tales to her children, her grandchildren, and to patients and clients she has served as a psychological social worker and marriage counselor.

This recently collected version of "Merrywise" is more than three times as long as the version Jane told at age eleven. One major set of additions to the tale as she tells it today is a wealth of specific details. These she attributes to her grandmother: "I realized that as I told as a young child, I probably left out a lot of the details. As I've gotten older, I remember the details. [My grandmother] was a very detailed person. She had artistic talent. She did pen and ink drawings, and . . . the drawings were all very tiny-lined."

A second major lengthening factor is the number and detail of the explanations that Jane gives in the later narrative. In her childhood version, Jane breaks into the narration with an evaluative comment only once: as the witch summons the animals of the forest, Jane states, "She screamed and cried and hollered (I guess her mouth was big enough)." Even this interjection is wryly indirect. The later version, however, is filled with explanations (for example, "keepsakes have a lot of magic," "people often used nightcaps when it was very cold in their houses," the pair of seven-mile-step boots "was a tool that witches had in those days"); some of these are clearly addressed to the listener ("surely by now you've figured that she was a witch"). Even more notable are the ways in which Jane details the qualities of Merrywise in her later telling, commenting on the hero's intelligence, curiosity, powers of observation, and listening skills.

Over the years, Jane has added many of these explanations to clarify the lessons for her own children and grandchildren, who did not hear the tales as often or identify with them as strongly as she did as a child. These variations from her grandmother's style come "from me. Because that's my way. When I tell my grandchildren, . . . they aren't me, going to their little own spot, pyschologically, with that. So I help to identify why Merrywise did the things he did."

The character Merrywise, clearly dominant in the story Jane told as a child, emerges as an even more powerful figure in the later version. For example, in eleven-year-old Jane's telling, as the boys flee the witch, each of them, apparently by his own motivation, throws out an object that magically grows into an obstacle for the witch. When sixty-two-year-old Jane retells the tale, it is Merrywise who directs his brothers to throw the objects. He is the sole brother to act with intelligence or courage anywhere in the tale.

Another important difference between the two tellings is the degree of subjectivity in the latter. In the earlier story, the young narrator describes events from an objective distance, only obliquely and partially inviting the listeners to experience the action as the characters do. For example, as Merrywise wakes up in the witch's bed in the middle of the night, young Jane explains, "Something was bothering him and he looked up and saw the old woman sitting on the edge of the bed." In the later telling, this twenty-word description is internalized and greatly expanded, as the listener is invited to follow the action through Merrywise's thoughts and senses: "He couldn't get to sleep, because he had all these troublements in his mind, and also because she snored. And so, she was sleeping and snoring, and snoring and sleeping, and then the snoring stopped. And he thought, 'Humm. Wonder what's going on here.' And he heard her just very, very quietly get up from the bed and go over to a place on a table in her room, and he could barely see in the darkened room, but she had something in her hand. And she came back to the bed. She sat down on the edge of the bed. . . . "

After Jane finished her tale, I asked her husband Bob if he had heard it before. He had not, though Jane's children and grandchildren had heard it many times. This fact is fully consonant with the tendency of contemporary Appalachian Märchen-tellers not only to keep their tales within the family, but also to confine their performances to private, intergenerational situations, as parent narrates to child, and grandparent to grandchild.

Jane's present performance style differs in some ways from the styles apparent on her early recordings. Having listened to many of Leonard Roberts's recordings of children from Jane's community, I would characterize their normative Märchen-telling style as reserved. The young narrators tend to perform in an almost deadpan monotone. Jane's 1949 performance of "Merrywise" generally partook of those basic qualities, though she tended to speak faster and more assuredly than the other children and to vary her intonation more. Roberts's later recordings of Jane, made in 1955, reveal a more demonstrative narrator, though still one whose style I would characterize as reserved, at least by the expressive standards of the storytelling revival of the late-twentieth century. When I played one of Jane's 1955 performances for her aunt, Glen Muncy Anderson, and asked her to compare it to Jane's grandmother's style, Glen stated that Jane's voicing, though similar to her grandmother's, was "more emphatic."

The performance of "Merrywise" recorded in 2000 is livelier than Jane's 1949 recording. Nevertheless, even as a sixty-two-year-old, she invests more energy in her word choice than in her intonation. She speaks a bit more softly and slowly than in her childhood narrations, but she varies her rhythm more and stresses more words. Toward the end of the tale, as the witch is pursuing the children, Jane speaks more quickly and adds colloquialisms, saying, for example, "git" instead of "get."

Carl Lindahl
University of Houston

"Merrywise"
as told by Jane Muncy, 1949[1]

Once upon a time there was a little boy and he had two brothers, Tom and Bill, and his name was Merrywise. And they lived in a little town, and their mother died. They didn't have nowhere to go and had no one to stay with. Their neighbor was a very kind woman and she asked Merrywise to stay with her while they went out to seek their fortune, but he wouldn't stay. So they were bound to take him with them. He went, and after they started they came to a house. They traveled for a long time and then they came to this house and knocked on the door. An old woman came to the door who had long hair. She had a long nose and she was real ugly. And he says, "May we stay all night here?"

And she said, "Yes, little boy. You're so cute I believe I'll let you be my little grandson."

And he said, "All right, granny."

So they went into the house and it came night. They got ready to lie down. And this old woman happened to be a witch. And she loved to kill people and she was going to kill Tom and Bill. So she put red caps on Tom and Bill and she had two boys, and she put white caps on her boys. And she told Merrywise he must sleep with her. So Merrywise and her laid down in the bed, and the boys laid down in the floor with their red caps and white caps on. Tom and Bill fell sound asleep and Merrywise did too. But in the middle of the night he woke up. Something was bothering him and he looked up and saw the old woman sitting on the edge of the bed. She was mumbling in a low voice, "I'll get up and whet my knife. I'll get up and whet my knife."

And then after he heard this he said, "I'll get up with you, granny."

She said, "No, you go back to bed."

And he said, "No, I'm not sleepy."

And she said, "I'll go with you."

And so they laid back down, and soon he heard her snore. He knew she was asleep. So he got up and kicked his brothers and woke them up, and changed the caps, and said, "You be ready to go when I wake you up, now."

So he went back to bed and started to snore, too, to pretend like he was asleep. And the old woman, which he called granny, woke up and set on the edge of the bed and begin to say, "I'll get up and whet my knife. I'll get up and whet my knife." He heard her, but really he pretended like he was asleep. So she thought he was asleep and she went over and looked at the boys which had the red caps on, and cut their heads off. She really thought it was Tom and Bill, but it was her boys. She went back to bed pleased and contented and laid down and went to sleep.

Merrywise got up just as soon as he heard her snore once more and kicked his brothers and they got up and went out. And as they came through the chicken yard Tom picked up an egg. As they came out the gate Bill picked up a rock, and as they got down the path Merrywise picked up a hickory nut. And they came on and traveled and traveled until it was almost the middle of the next day. But the woman had not found out until then that it was her boys she had killed and not Tom and Bill. So she made a storm and put on her seven-mile-step boots and started after them. Soon she gained up with them, and when she did she said, "I'll get you this time."

And then Bill threw down his rock and a great rock wall came around her. She cried and cried and screamed for all of the beasts in the forest to come and beat a hole big enough for her to crawl through. And after a few days they did, and they got a hole beat through so she could come. She crawled through the hole and started out again with her seven-mile-steps, seven-mile-steps, seven-mile-steps.

And pretty soon she caught up with them again. Then Bill threw down his egg and a great river of egg yellow came around her. And she couldn't even see the shore, so she screamed and cried and hollered (I guess her mouth was big enough) for all the beasts of the forest to hear and they came and licked a path big enough for her to come through, and she came through. And then she went on. So she soon caught up with them with her seven-mile-step boots, and Merrywise threw down his hickory nut. A great forest of hickory trees come up and the boys climbed up a tree. And she says, "Well, if you're going to do that I can too." So they ran up the tree and she ran up the tree after them. They ran down the other side, and she ran down the other side and they ran back up. And she said, "I won't fool with you any more. My legs are rusted and I won't run up the tree after you any more."

So she took out a bag, a funny looking bag, out of her pocket and opened it up and said, "Bill, jump down in my puddin-tuddin bag!"

And Bill said, "All right." So he jumped down into the bag.

And then she said, "Tom, jump down in my puddin-tuddin bag." And Tom jumped down. And she said, "Merrywise, jump down in my puddin-tuddin bag."

And he says, "I won't do it, granny. I don't obey you."

And she says, "Well, I'll come up after you." She came up and he went down, and it went on like that for a while, and she got tired. And he got down first. He pulled his brothers out of the bag, and opened it up and said, "Granny, jump down into my puddin-tuddin bag." And she jumped down, and they put rocks in the bag and tied her up and threw her in the river and killed her. And they went back to their house and lived happy ever after.

Note

1. Jane Muncy's 1949 telling of Merrywise was transcribed and edited by Leonard Roberts and later printed as tale 10a in his *South from Hell-fer-Sartin* (Lexington: University of Kentucky Press, 1955:42–45). Copyright 1955 by the University of Kentucky Press. Reprinted by permission of the University Press of Kentucky. All rights reserved.

"Merrywise"
as told by Jane Muncy Fugate, June 3, 2000

When I would ask [my grandmother] for favorite stories, they would sometimes be the Jack tales. The names of, the names of the people in her stories: they generally were about young men. And the names would be Tom, and Bill, and either Jack or—my favorite story was "Merrywise." And when I look at the name "Merrywise," you know, he was not only the hero who was the youngest, but he was smarter than Tom and Bill. And could figure out things that they couldn't figure out. And so, the message to me was, you can be little, and you can be frail, and you can be the youngest, and you can be alone, but you can also be the smartest. And the "Merrywise"—"merry" meaning "happy"—you could be happy. You could be happy and you could be wise, and you can overcome. And so I thought of myself as that overcomer.

> Carl Lindahl: I've, I've heard you on tapes, long-ago tapes, telling at least three stories of someone named Merrywise. Among those, was there one that was a favorite—that you could remember right now?

I, I think probably my *favorite* Merrywise story was about Merrywise, and he changed from time to time—little pieces of information came in and out about him—but he was the youngest and he was, his siblings were Tom and Bill. And Tom and Bill were not all that—they were not all that sharp. But Merrywise was as sharp as a tack.

They had been orphaned, and had been living with a neighbor, friend and neighbor. And the neighbor was getting old and it was time for Tom and Bill and Merrywise to go out in the world and seek their fortune. Now, that was never really explained in the stories, about seeking fortune. It was just something that when you got old enough, you went out to do.

So Tom and Bill told the little old lady they'd been living with, "We're going out to seek our fortunes." And Merrywise said, "I want to go, too."

And the little old lady said, "You're too young, Merrywise. You can't go."

And Merrywise said, "But I'm going." And so he prevailed and out they went, the three boys, Tom and Bill and Merrywise, to seek their fortune. And they had very, very little, just enough to have for lunch. But on their way out of the yard of the person they'd been living with, they each picked up a keepsake. And little did they know, but there was magic in the keepsake. And keepsakes have a lot of magic anyway— they, they do a lot of wonderful things for people who keep them.

So Tom picked up a rock, and he put it in his pocket. Just a small— nothing spectacular—just a rock.

Bill picked up an egg as he went past the henhouse. He reached in and grabbed a fresh egg and he put it in his pocket.

And Merrywise, who *always* loved nature and growing things, picked up an acorn from the oak tree and he put it in his pocket with loving care.

And off they went to seek their fortunes. And they did have lunch with them. The lunch was wrapped up in the knapsack, and they took that apart and they ate that, and they went on and on and on through the woods until it was nighttime. And they were growing quite tired and quite hungry. And guess what? There was a light shining through the trees and Merrywise was the first to spot it of course, since he was awful observant, and he said, "Look, brothers, there's a light. There must be someone living at that house."

And so they went up the path into the house and knocked on the door. And inside the house there was a woman. They heard her coming to the door and she opened the door, and *my, oh my,* she was ugly. She had a long nose and a sharp chin and scraggly hair, and she was dressed in dowdy, long, loose clothing. And she said to them—she looked at them and she rubbed her hands together and . . . she said, "And who have we here?"

And Tom said, "My name is Tom," and Bill said, "My name is Bill," and Merrywise said, "I'm Merrywise."

And she said, "Well, what would you have here, boys?"

And they said, "We are tired and we are hungry, and we wonder if we could spend the night?"

And then she said, "Well, certainly," and she rubbed her hands together. "Come on in. I have two boys of my own."

And so they saw these scraggly looking, waif-y looking, almost-as-ugly-as-she-was people sitting in the corner, but they went on in and she fed them, and she said to them, "Now my boys sleep up in the attic, and so I'll just make you a pallet on the other side, and you two boys can sleep up there with my two boys, and this little fella here, he can sleep with me."

And so Merrywise didn't know if he liked that or not. He was used to sleeping in the family bed situation, but he didn't like the looks of her much and didn't trust her much, and beside that, when he—she took the brothers upstairs, she said to her two boys, "Now, boys, you put on these white caps" (because people often used nightcaps when it was very cold in their houses, and particularly if you slept in an attic, or a loft). And she said to Tom and Bill, "*You* two boys put on these *red* nightcaps." And he saw that she was pretty definite about that and wondered why that was. He was a boy with great curiosity. In addition to being one who noted his surroundings, he was curious about his surroundings.

So she said to him, "Now, come on, little fella, you come down and you sleep with me, and we'll be warm." And he does what he's told, but he couldn't get to sleep, because he had all these troublements in his mind, and also because she snored.

And so, she was sleeping and snoring, and snoring and sleeping, and then the snoring stopped. And he thought, "Humm. Wonder what's going on here." And he heard her just very, very quietly get up from the bed and go over to a place on a table in her room, and he could *barely* see in the darkened room, but she had something in her hand.

And she came back to the bed. She sat down on the edge of the bed, and she said, [chanting] "I'll get up and whet my knife. I'll get up and whet my knife." (Well, whetting is sharpening, as everybody knows.) And so Merrywise, who was this curious, interested little guy— also not very trusting toward her at this point—wondered what she was whetting her knife for after she'd gone to bed and gone to sleep. Humm?

So he said to her, as he popped up, "What are you doing, Granny? What are you doing with that knife?"

"I'm not doing anything. Now, you go back down and go to sleep. I'm just up here fixing this, and I'll be back to bed in just a minute here. Just getting ready for the breakfast in the morning. You come back and go to sleep."

And so she got back in the bed, and she was very still and quiet, and he decided that he would *pretend* that he went asleep and he would watch. And so, as he was pretending to be asleep, sort of breathing hard so she'd think he was sleeping, up she got again, and in a lower voice, very definitely he heard her speak, [whispering]

"I'll get up and whet my knife
I'll get up and whet my knife—"

So she did that. She whetted her knife, and when he figured that knife must be pretty sharp, she left the room.

So he followed her. And up she went, carefully, carefully up the attic stairs, to the loft, taking her knife, without its cover, *obviously* going to use it. And he saw her. And she sat in the corner and said,

"I'll get up and whet my knife
I'm going to whet my knife—"

He stole past her very carefully, and changed the nightcaps of the two sets of boys while she sharpened her knife, facing in a different direction.

And here she comes, over to the bedside of the guys in the red caps, and *lopped* off their heads, right there, in front of him. And goes away, chuckling to herself, back down the stairs. Oh my, that was scary for Merrywise, and he stayed hidden in the shadows, and as soon as she went downstairs, he kicked his brothers hard ones in the rear and he said to them, "Get up, Tom! Get up here, Bill! We got to get out of this place quick, quick before she finds out she's made a mistake."

And so sleepy eyed and sort of dumbfounded, the brothers got up and they followed little Merrywise out the window, and down the nearest tree limb, grabbing their clothes as they went. And off they went. Out into the darkness again.

Well, the witch—because surely by now you figured out she was a witch and was up to no good—probably intended to eat those boys, or at least keep Merrywise until he was fat enough. And off they went, and she went and—

[Tape recorder stops; Jane refers to the break in narration as she picks up the thread of her tale.]

Well, it is time for part two, because that's when the adventure began.

She waited till morning. Realized that little Merrywise wasn't in bed, of course, but went up and found her two sons with the *wrong* nightcaps on, beheaded. Oh, was she mad. She was enraged, and she developed the worst witch self she could muster up. And she went to her hiding place, and got out her seven-mile-step boots. Now that was a tool that witches had in those days. They could put certain boots, and they not only could not only take a step, they could take seven miles at one step, or whatever they had it programmed for.

Well, she took out after these boys. And they had a good bit of the night to travel, and so they were running as fast as their little wayward legs could carry them, off into the distance, trying to get away from her.

And Merrywise—who, by the way, had very good hearing—in addition to being smart, in addition to being curious—he was gifted with exceptional hearing. And so he stopped and listened and he heard her off in the distance, and she coming: seven-mile-a-step, seven-mile-a-step. And he could hear that she was really angry and she was *very close* at that point.

And so he said to his brothers, "Oh, brothers. Here she comes. She's close. We've got to do something. Tom, throw down your magic keepsake."

And so Tom reached in his pocket and grabbed the rock and he *threw* it down, and instantly it changed into a beautiful, tall, *unmountable* stone wall that just blocked off where she was from where they were. So there they were behind it—taking off again and running as fast as they could.

And she came up to it. Now she had great powers as a witch, but she realized a stone wall she couldn't get over and she couldn't go through. But she *could* command some help. And so she yelled, "All the animals in the world, all the animals in the world! Come to me and come to me now. And I want you to use your hoofs and your horns, and I want you to make a hole in this wall."

And as they were commanded, all the animals in the world came and they started hoofing away at that wall, and butting it with their horns, and making a hole. And pretty soon, as the hours went by, she was able to get through the rock.

Well, little Merrywise, with his ears and cunning hearing, he could hear kind of what was going on, and because he was smart he guessed what was going on and, and he could hear her again begin with the "Seven-mile-a-step, seven-mile a step, I'm going to catch those boys, and when I do, they're gone. They're goners for sure. Seven-mile-a-step," and she was upon them again.

And Tom was shivering with fear and Bill practically peed his pants, he was so scared. And she said to him—she said to them, "I'm going to git you this time. I've got you this time!"

And Merrywise said, "Bill, throw down your magic keepsake. And so Bill reached in his pocket and took out the egg, and he threw down the egg, and it turned into a giant lake of egg. Thick and gooey, and big—and hard to get through even for a witch.

And so the boys took off running again, as fast as they could go. Merrywise kickin em in the butt, making em go faster, running as fast as he could. And the witch was on the other side of the egg lake.

And she knew she couldn't get through that big huge swamp, egg lake, by herself, but she did, had witch's powers and so once again she screamed out into the world, "All the animals of the world, all the animals of the world, *come* to help me." And when they did, she said, "Lick a hole in this lake, enough for me to get through. Give me a path because I've got to go after these boys. I'll git them and I'll git them for good this time." And so all the animals in the world—a bunch of animals *do* like eggs—but she had commanded them, and they began to lick and lick and lick and lick, and finally there was a pathway where the witch could walk through. And she did.

And the seven-mile-a-step boots got all gummy and gooey and *may* have been put out of operation at that time, but she did catch up with the boys pretty much as quickly as she could. And she was growlin and snarlin and usin words to them that she was gonna get em, that she was gonna get em for sure.

And so Merrywise said, "Don't be afraid, boys. Just follow me." And he took out his acorn keepsake, from his pocket. No doubt it was the greatest magic of all. And he *threw* it down and up from the acorn sprung an oak tree—full grown, tall, lanky, climbable oak tree.

And so up the oak tree they went. Tom went first, and then went Bill, and then went Merrywise, until they climbed to the very top of the tree, *just* as the wicked old woman came to the bottom of the tree.

And she shook her fist at em, and she said, "I'll git you yet. I've got something you can't get away from. I'll get my Puddin-Tuddin Bag." And so she took out from inside her bosom, where everybody carries really important things, a bag that she unfolded, that was her Puddin-Tuddin Bag. Well, it too was magic. And she opened it up, and she said to Bill, who was leaning out looking over the tree, "Bill! Jump into my Puddin-Tuddin Bag this minute."

And Bill just took flight, and off he went, off the branch and—plunk!—down into the Puddin-Tuddin Bag. And Merrywise thought, "Oh, look at that stupid brother of mine!"

And she said to Tom, who was looking out over his branch of the tree, "Tom! Jump immediately into this Puddin-Tuddin Bag, because I say so. Into the Puddin-Tuddin Bag!"

And Tom took flight off the end of the branch—plunk! Whoosh! Landed on his brother inside the Puddin-Tuddin Bag, and he too was in the bag.

And so she *packed* them down inside the bag, and she now grinned with a great big toothless grin, at Merrywise, and said, "Merrywise! Because I say you should, jump into this Puddin-Tuddin Bag with your brothers right now!"

And he said, "No way, Granny. I'm not coming into your Puddin-Tuddin Bag. I won't do it. I will not come into your Puddin-Tuddin Bag. I'm not coming. You'll have to come and get me."

And so up the tree she came, and he ran down the tree. And kicked the boys in the bag, and said, "Get out of that bag, you lazy, stupid brothers of mine. Get out of that bag. You've got to run."

But he didn't get em out of there in time. They were hesitant because she commanded it. And she got back down the tree, and up they all went up the tree again.

And so she said, cackling to herself, "I'll get you this time, boys! She opened up her bag, and said, "Tom, jump into my Puddin-Tuddin Bag!" And right off the limb he went again.

Didn't learn from his mistakes.

And she said, "Bill, jump into my Puddin-Tuddin Bag." And right off he went again, and right into the Puddin-Tuddin Bag: splat, right on his brother, and down in the bag.

And she said, "Merrywise, this time *you* jump into my Puddin-Tuddin Bag, right now. Because I'm going to git you."

And Merrywise said, "No. I won't. You come up and get me." And so this time, he went back down the tree as she came up speedier than ever. He kicked his brothers harder than ever, he dumped the bag out, and out they came, and just as she got to the top of the tree, he opened up the bag and said to his brothers, "You sit there. Don't move." And he opened up the bag, and he said, "Granny, old wicked witch! Jump into this Puddin-Tuddin Bag right now, because I command you now." And off the top of the limb she went, floating through the air, coming down headfirst—plunk! Right into the Puddin-Tuddin Bag.

And Merrywise was ready for that, because he'd seen this thing twice, and another thing about Merrywise is, he learned from his mistakes. And he wasn't going to let her get away at the end. And so he squooshed her down into that bag and tied around the drawstrings as tight as he could tie em, and wrapped em around and put a big knot in it, and he watched her punching around in that bag. And he said, "Got to get something in here." And so he sent Tom and Bill, who were sitting there with their mouths hanging open, "Go to the creek quick, and get some rocks!" And they went to the creek, deep creek that came into the mouth of a river that was also very deep, and he said, "Pick up rocks." They did, and they brought the rocks back. They were pretty big, heavy rocks, altogether weighing almost as much as the witch herself. Quickly he untied the drawstrings. Quickly he opened it up, barely, and they threw in the rocks. They tied the drawstrings back again fast as they could. And there she was with rocks in the bag.

Now they knew they had to get rid of her. But I forgot to tell you something very important. This old lady never traveled without her bag of gold. And the bag of gold—when she tried to get the boys in the Puddin-Tuddin Bag, of course, she sat down the bag of gold, so that she could have both hands to hold the Puddin-Tuddin Bag open. And all this running up and down the tree and running down the tree and jumping in the bag and jumping at em and getting out of the bag, and all of that. All of that—and the bag of gold had gone unnoticed. Just like I almost forgot to tell you about it.

Well, after they had her tied, and they were going to take her down to the creek of course—'cause that's what people did with unwanted things. They took em to the creek and tied em up in a bag and, and— you know, like an unwanted litter of puppies or kittens, or some other, fiendish thing that might hurt you, you put it in a bag, you tied it up, and you threw it in a river or a creek.

And so the three boys dragged her down there—and plunk! Splat! . . . Plunk! Gloop, gloop, gloop—down she went. To the bottom.

And the creek, that was kind of free-flowing, just washed her right on down to the mouth of the big river, and of course she couldn't get out of the bag. She couldn't call for anybody, and everybody knows you can drown witches. So, as the boys watched it happen and knew she was gone, they realized that they didn't want to go back to their house. They couldn't go back to where they'd started from, because they were out to seek their fortune after all, but they passed by the tree, the oak tree. And there, on a root of the oak tree, sat the bag of gold. Oh, my—the bag of gold. And so they looked inside of it, and figured out that there was enough fortune there for all of them to live from here on, and they probably could get really really pretty wives, and they probably could have great farms and terrific lives, and live happy ever after.

And so they, they did just that. They divided up the gold and they went off and they lived happy ever after. And nobody ever heard from that old witch again.

Two Versions of "Rawhead and Bloodybones" from the Farmer-Muncy Family

These two tales, told by aunt and niece, respectively, in 1997 and 2000, illustrate how individual response to a single story—learned from the same teller—can vary even within the same family. The original narrator of "Rawhead and Bloodybones" was Sidney Farmer Muncy, mother of Glen Muncy Anderson and grandmother of Jane Muncy Fugate.

A comparison of these two tales with a third performance from the same family—a version told by Jane, age 11, in 1949 and published in Leonard Roberts's *South from Hell-fer-Sartin* (1955)—reveals a remarkable number of major differences, particularly in the early episodes of each. In all three versions, a wicked stepmother sends her angelic stepdaughter on a quest to retrieve water from a distant place in hopes that the child will never return. In Glen Muncy Anderson's telling, the girl encounters a hungry dog that asks her for food; when she has fed the dog, it becomes her magic helper. In Jane Muncy's 1949 performance, the stepmother seeks the aid of a witch, who sets traps to destroy her stepdaughter; however, once the girl has shared her food with an old man, she receives his help and proceeds unharmed to the well. In Jane's 2000 performance, the witch has disappeared from the tale, but the old man remains as the donor who helps the girl reach her destination.

The three vastly different tales become much more similar once the girl has reached the goal of her quest. In all three, the stepdaughter encounters creatures named Rawhead and Bloodybones. In all three, each creature asks the girl to "wash me, and dry me, and lay me down easy" (or uses words very similar to these). After the stepdaughter does so, she is rewarded with physical beauty, a beautiful fragrance, and gold and silver, which fall from her hair when she combs it after returning home. In all three versions, the stepmother, greedy for more gold, sends her own daughter (or daughters, in Jane's 2000 version) on a quest for more water. But the daughter refuses to share her food or to wash the Rawhead and Bloodybones. Thus she is cursed with an evil odor, ugliness, and a host of vermin that fall from her hair when she combs it.

Both Glen and Jane retained sharp mental images of the Rawhead and Bloodybones. There seems to be a correlation between the two narrators' vivid impressions of the Rawhead and Bloodybones and the fact that their greatly different stories begin to run closely parallel as soon as these creatures appear. Although both Glen and Jane were deeply

affected by their images of the Rawhead and Bloodybones, they differed
greatly in their responses to those images. Glen remembers the story
most vividly from her early childhood in the 1910s; for her, the tale was
a horrific experience that evoked vivid and terrifying memories. Jane
first heard the story about thirty years later, when she also was a young
child. To Jane, "Rawhead and Bloodybones" was anything but terrifying; she regarded the story as a special, loving gift from her grandmother.
The two women's responses to "Rawhead and Bloodybones" are discussed
at greater length in my essay "Sounding a Shy Tradition" (this volume).

Although Glen modestly downplayed her talents as a storyteller, she
demonstrated considerable narrative skill in the course of my visit when
telling a number of personal and family tales. In the comments recorded
below, Glen hints at a preference for true stories as well as stories in
which her listeners can identify themselves, such as the tales she made
up for her children. Glen's performance of "Rawhead and Bloodybones"
is strongest when it is most personal. For example, hers is the only one
of the three versions that identifies the daughter and stepdaughter by
name, and Glen has named the evil daughter "Suzy," after a girl she
disliked when she was a child. Glen narrates "Rawhead and Bloodybones"
in an even and unemphatic tone, though she occasionally breaks into
snatches of dialogue toward the end of the tale, as when the cruel stepmother says to the heroine, "Comb it yourself," and the evil daughter
tells the little dog, "Go find you something to eat." Such lines are delivered in an abrupt and dismissive tone, providing effective jolts in an
otherwise smooth performance.

I [CL] recorded Glen Muncy Anderson's version of "Rawhead and
Bloodybones" on May 4, 1997, at the home she shares with her sister,
Hope Muncy [HM], who was also present for the performance. The
women are daughters of Mrs. Sidney Farmer Muncy and aunts of Jane
Muncy Fugate.

Jane told *her* version of the story on June 3, 2000, in her home. This
version differs substantially from the story she told Leonard Roberts in
1949, when she was eleven years old. As noted earlier, the two performances diverge significantly at the outset, but begin to run parallel when
the heroine encounters the Rawhead and Bloodybones. After this point,
Jane's later performance differs from the earlier by adding numerous
details, most notably an extensive dialogue among the Rawhead and
Bloodybones, who discuss with each other the various wishes they be-
stowed upon the heroine. The only major plot change occurs at the
end. The tale told in 1949 concluded much like that of her Aunt Glen,
with the snakes and frogs and other vermin spilling from the wicked
girls' hair and running off the stepmother. To this image, the eleven-
year-old narrator added only a brief coda: "And her stepdaughter lived

happy ever after, there with her money." The later version, however, concludes with a prince and a marriage.

As in her performance of "Merrywise" (this volume), Jane begins "Rawhead and Bloodybones" in a relatively even and unemphatic voice that grows more demonstrative toward the end. When the heroine reaches the water at the end of the world, Jane begins to add characterizing emphasis; this is particularly notable in the dialogue in which the Rawhead and Bloodybones discuss their wishes for the heroine. Also, as the heroine returns home with her beauty and fragrance enhanced, Jane emphasizes the girl's transformation by having the townspeople speak in tones of wonder: such lines as "*What* is that smell?" are delivered with significant vocal stress. Like her aunt Glen, Jane also intensifies the negative portrayal of the wicked stepmother and her daughters by adding emphasis and a scornful tone to lines of dialogue such as, "*No*, I won't comb your hair, you lazy thing!"

Carl Lindahl
University of Houston

"Rawhead and Bloodybones"
as told by Glen Muncy Anderson, May 4, 1997

CL: You were telling me something before I turned on the tape recorder that I, I found very interesting—that when your mother told these stories, they would scare you.

GMA: Scare me to *death*. I would stay over on my—I had a pull-out bed, you know. And then she had these two beds. And I would sleep on that for awhile, and then I'd get so scared that I crawled—get up and crawl across the floor and get in the bed with her. I'd get at the foot of the bed. And Mark and Gill had the bed over. *They* would get out and they'd come. And Mark and I would be at the foot, and she would be up there, Hope would be on one side and Gill was little bitty, he was two. We were two, four, and six, like that.

CL: So you remember this from a very long time ago?

GMA: Yes.

CL: This is an early memory?

GMA: Yes, but I tried to forget em. The stories would scare me. And I didn't tell em to my children. I said, "No, I won't tell that." I read to them. I was—we had children's books and things. Each night we had our story hour. One would get on one side and one on the other side, and they'd stand behind. Even the larger girls that I had—the three large ones would come. I would read before they went to bed.

And then the little ones, their bedtime stories—I would tell them stories—funny stories or good stories, about what they did, and I'd tell a story and have their names in it, you know. Make up stories. Which I wish I'd have remembered [laughing].

CL: [Referring to a tape-recording of "Tailipoe," a gruesome tale told by Glen's niece Jane Muncy to Leonard Roberts. I had played the tape for Glen and Hope earlier that day.] So here I thought I was doing you a treat by playing you that story, but it was probably one of the stories that scared you when you were a kid.

GMA: I'm all right now. [laughs]

CL: Okay. Well, I didn't mean to bring up anything like that. [laughter]

GMA: I'm all right now. [laughs] Because I know—at the time I thought they were *real*. You know, children think—things are real to them. They—you have to tell them it's make believe or what. Just like on the, on the television sometimes it gets so graphic that the children will think it's real, and you have to tell them that that's not real—or not let them see it. . . .

There was one that my mother told, "Rawhead and Bloodybones." Oh, that was awful. . . .

There was a woman that had—there was always a bad stepmother, you know. Always. And the man had died, and he had a beautiful girl. Little girl. Mary. And he married this widow woman that had a ugly little girl, and her name—I always called her Suzy, because I didn't like a little girl named Suzy, so the bad one was Suzy. So, Suzy.

The mother said, "Now, you go to the well, Mary, and take a big bucket and bring back some water." And it was a long way to the well.

So little Mary went along and she saw a little dog. And, by the way, the stepmother gave her a biscuit for her lunch, if she got hungry.

And the dog says, "I'm hungry."

And she said, "You can have half of my biscuit." And she gave the little dog half the biscuit.

And the dog says, "Thank you. I hope you smell good the rest of your life."

So she went on a little farther and there was an old lady she met. And the old lady said, "I'm old, and I can't get around very well, and I need help, and I'm hungry."

And she said, "You can have the rest of my lunch." And she took her by the arm and she led her over and set her down on the, a bank.

And the old woman said, "I hope that—you are beautiful now, and I hope you are beautifuller—you get beautiful, more beautiful each day."

So she went on to the well. And there she heard something, and she looked and there was Rawhead and Bloodybones.

[HM chuckles.]

And, it said, "Wash me off and dry me off and turn me over easy."

So she washed it off and dried it off and turned it over easy. And it said, "I hope, when you comb your hair, you'll have gold come out of your hair."

So she went back to the house and with the water. And the step-mother said, "Why are you so long getting back?"

And she told about helping the people on the way and what she did. And she said, "My head itches. Will you comb my hair?"

And the stepmother said, "Comb it yourself."

And she set down and combed it, and out come money. All that gold came out.

And the stepmother said, "What is that smells so good?" And it was the little girl.

And she said, "You look different from, than you did." And she was so beautiful.

And so she said, "I'm going to send my daughter back." She fixed a lunch basket, with all goodies in it, and gave her a little pail and told her to go to the well.

And the little girl went by, and she saw the old dog. And the dog said, "Oh, I'm hungry."

And she said, "Go find you something to eat. I'm going to eat all my food myself. It's just enough for me."

So the little dog went on to say, "You smell bad now and I hope you smell worse the rest of your life."

And she went on. She met the old lady. And the old lady said, "I'm old and I can't get around very well. Will you help me?"

And she said, "Help yourself. I've got other things to do. Just help yourself."

And the old lady said, "You're ugly now, and I hope you're uglier the rest of your life."

And she went on to the well, and she heard something say—groaning—and she looked and it was Rawhead and Bloodybones. And she said, uh, it said: "Wash me off, dry me off, and turn me over easy."

And she said, "Wash your own old self off. I've got other things to do." And she kind of kicked it out of the way, and she got the little bucket, and she went skipping back home.

And the stepmother said, "What is that smells like that?" And it was the little girl.

And she says, "What's happened to you?" She was so ugly.

And she said, "My head itches—(Oh yeah, Bloodybones said, "I hope that when you comb your hair, you'll have nothing but snakes and frogs in your hair.")

So the grandmother [sic] said, "Oh come here, honey, and let me comb your hair in my lap." And she combed her hair, and out come snakes and frogs, and snakes and frogs.

End of the story. I don't know the rest of it. There's no more to it. It always ended like that.

Can you see why that would scare a little four-year-old girl sleeping off in the corner by herself?

"Rawhead and Bloodybones"
as told by Jane Muncy Fugate, June 3, 2000

Well, "Rawhead and Bloodybones" started in a kingdom far away. There was a girl who had been left with her wicked stepmother. The father had brought his daughter into the marriage and the wicked stepmother was in charge of her while father was away. Well, he didn't come back. And so, this young girl lived in the family pretty much abused by her sister and—I think my grandmother would have said she was "treated hatefully by her stepmother and her stepsisters." If there was a hard chore to do on the place, they sent her to do it. If there was something that was dirty and nobody else wanted to do, she did. She was very obedient. Quite beautiful in her way, if you could look through the dirt and the ragged clothes, because she was not allowed to have the finery of her two sisters. And she wished and wished and wished that she could live with her father and her mother, but it wasn't to be. Her mother was long dead and her father was away and not returning. So she had kind of a hard life. And one day her wicked stepmother said to her, "You know, I think what would make myself and my daughters around here [happy], would be a, a bucket from the end of the world. So I want you to take this bucket and I want you to go to the end of the world and collect a bucket full of water and bring it back for us to drink. And be on with you now!"

And so a tired, forlorn little girl said, "But, Stepmother dear, I don't have anything to eat on this long journey, and you know it's a long journey to the end of the world." And the stepmother said, "Now, git you a biscuit on the way out, and don't bother me anymore." So off she went, carrying the bucket to the end of the world.

And as you know, it's a long trip to the end of the world. So she traveled and traveled and traveled and the day got hot, and all she had to eat was the biscuit, but she waited as long as she could and when her stomach was rumbling and she was really hungry, she sat down under a nice and friendly tree and opened up her little kerchief that had the biscuit inside it, and started to eat it.

Well, about that time, a voice came from the back of the tree, and there was a little old man, and he *did* look strange, but friendly. And he said to her, "Young woman, pretty girl, would you mind sharing your dinner with me?" (Dinner was a word that was used for lunch). And so she said, "Well, I'll, I'll share my dinner with you. I don't have very much, but you can have it." And so she broke her biscuit and she gave him the biggest half and they sat there and ate it together and he said to her, "Well, where are you going?"

She said, "I'm going to the end of the world, and I'm going to draw a bucket of water from the end of the world, and I'm going to come back, and I'm going to give it to my stepmother and my sisters."

And he said, "Well, I hope you have a lot of good luck, and I know you'll do fine, because it seems like you're a good person."

And she said, "Thank you very much." So she took herself up off the tree where she'd been resting and she left the little old man and he pulled his cap down over his eyes and off she went trudging down the road, carrying the bucket.

And just as she was going out of sight, he said, "Oh, my, what a nice, what a good girl that was. Ah, she will have her some good luck, she will."

And so she trudges on, and on and on and on and keeps going on until the end of the world is finally in sight. And, sure enough, there's the big, big river at the end of the world. So she took her bucket, and she plunged it down into the deep, murky water and drew it up, with its rope. And she looked down inside and there was this funny-looking thing, and she looked closer at it inside, and then she poured some of the water off of it, and it began to talk to her, and it said, "Dump me out and wash me, and dry me, and lay me down easy." And it was Rawhead and Bloodybones.

She felt so sorry for it that she did just that, she took it very carefully out of the bucket, and she washed it, dried it, put it in the sun so gently. And put her bucket back down in the water. Puzzled as she was, she put her bucket down in the water, and pulled it up again thinking she was going to get a bucket of water, and sure enough, there inside of it was another one of those things, and it too talked to her and it said, "Please dump me out, wash me and dry me and lay me down easy." So she said "okay" and she carefully turned it out onto the bank, and washed it and dried it, and *so* gently, she put it in the sunshine to dry. And it was just laid there soaking up the sun. So she was really puzzled now, but she put her bucket back down in the water and drew it up again, from even a deeper place this time, and sure enough there was another, a third Rawhead and Bloodybones. And it too spoke to her, and it said, "Wash me and dry me and lay me down easy." So she did that. She washed it and dried it, turned it out into the sun, beside the two other ones, and all in a row they sat, soaking up the sun. Looking comfortable.

So she said, "I *do hope* that this time I could get my bucket full of water, because I know they're going to be looking for me back home." She put a bucket in, and this time it came up with the water—a little murky, because the-end-of-the-world water is murky, but it—she got the water and started home with her bucket.

And a bucket full of the-end-of-the-world water is heavy, but she was strong because she'd been doing a lot of work, and so she made it back. Took a long time to get back to her home, but as she came to the village, she was coming closer and closer, and some strange things began to happen. And it was all as a result of what had been going back on at the riverbank. Because as she walked away, the first Rawhead and Bloodybones said, "Well, she was pretty and she was kind. But I wish for her that she be the most beautiful girl in the world, so beautiful that people are just amazed when they look at her."

"Um. That's a good wish," said the second Rawhead and Bloodybones. "Well, she smelled good, even though she'd been walking; she had a sweet smell about her, and she was kind, and she did smell good. And you know what I wish? I wish that from here on, she smelled like a thousand flowers all in a group, and that when people saw, they were amazed, not only by her beauty, but by how good she smelled."

"Yay," they said, "that's good wishing. Good job, good job."

And so the third Rawhead and Bloodybones, he said, "Well, okay. I wish that she is beautiful and that she does smell pretty, but I also wish that when she gets back home, that her hair will grow very heavy when it needs to be combed, and that when she combs through her hair, that diamonds and pearls and gold will come falling out on the floor. Heaps, large heaps of riches. And she will be wealthy, and wealthy forevermore."

"Oh, good job," they all said. "We like it. Yes." And so our heroine walks back to her community. And as she gets to the outside of the town, where the outside-town people live, they all start to open their windows, and they poke out their heads and they'd say, *"What* is that smell?" And then they see her. And they say, "Oh, my goodness, did you ever see anyone so beautiful? Ah, she takes away your breath, and she's so beautiful." Every house she passes by on the road, the same thing. They're just amazed.

And so by the time she comes into town, there's a clamor at the edge of town. And the sisters come out to see what the clamor's all about, and the stepmother comes out to see what the clamor's all about and there she is. And she's *positively* beautiful. And so she sees that they are all amazed at her, and *she* is amazed at how they're treating her. But she comes into the house and she says to her wicked stepmother, who is standing there looking at her beauty and smelling her sweet smell, and she says, "Oh, Stepmother dear," she says. "My head feels so heavy and so tired from my trip. And I brought you your water from the end of the world." She says, "Could you please comb out my long, golden hair for me?"

And the stepmother says, *"No,* I won't comb your hair, you lazy thing! You comb your own hair."

And so she gets the comb, and she begins to comb out her hair, and out fall thousands of *beautiful,* perfect pearls. And out come diamonds falling in a heap around her feet. And out comes gold, splattering and rolling around the floor. Riches untold, to make a person rich for the rest of their life.

And so the stepmother, who was not only wicked, but greedy—which is one of the things that you have when you're wicked—said, "Where did this come from?"

And she said, "I don't know. I don't know. I don't know."

And so the stepmother says, "Girls! Daughters of mine. Come here, come here right away. You get this bucket. You get this bucket. You go to the end of the world, and you come back with a bucket of water from the end of the world, and you better bring back some stuff in your hair too, girls. Because I want all these riches. We'll take hers, and we'll take theirs, and we'll—we're going to be rich."

And so they said, "We don't want to go, Mother"—because they were lazy—and "We don't want to do that."

And she said, "You go, and you get out of here right now." And she kicks them in the butt. She gives them—but she says, "But I'm going to fix you a big lunch." So she wraps up in a checkered table-cloth, oh the nicest of meats—venison—and the greatest of breads from her larder, and pie, and she fixes them a *great* meal for their journey. And so off they go to the end of the world—grumbling and mumbling and fussing. And they do *not* want to do this trip. And they're fighting with each other, and elbowin each other and kicking each other and kicking stones, and fighting over who's going to carry the knapsack, and it got to be that time of day when they were going to sit down to eat. And there was the beautiful tree.

So they each picked a root (they wanted each other's, of course, because they were that way, they were cantankerous), but they finally found their roots and they sat down and they opened this *gorgeous* meal in front of them. And they were *gobbling* it up and shoving it in their mouths and fighting over the last bits and morsels, and from around the side of the back of the tree, they hear a voice. And they saw a little old man, funny looking—and he says, "Girls? Girls? Hello. I'm hungry, and I wonder if you could share your dinner with me?"

And they said, "Ah! Who are you? You look funny. We don't want you touching our food. Get away from here! No, we won't share with you. Who do you think you are? Get away from here, get out, be *gone.*"

And so he slinked off, and went over beside another tree, and sort of disappeared behind it. And they ate their fill and they napped for awhile, and they quarreled with each other, and then they got back up and got out on the path to the end of the world.

And they walked and they walked and they quarreled and they walked, and it was getting almost dark by the time that they got to the end of the world. "I don't know why we have to make this trip. I hate this trip and I hate being with you."

"I don't know why we had to make this trip either, and I don't want to carry an old big full bucket of water home when I go home."

And so, the first daughter, she put down her bucket into the deep and murky water, and she drew it up, and guess who was there? I bet you guessed—it was the Rawhead and Bloodybones. So he said to her, "Will you dump me out carefully, wash me, dry me, and lay me down easy?"

And she said, "*Ah!* No, I won't. Git!" She threw him back in the water.

And so the other daughter, Number Two, said, "Huh! You can't do anything right." She put her bucket down into the water, and she drew it up, and there was the second Rawhead and Bloodybones. And he said, "Wash me and dry me and lay me down easy."

And she said, "Get away!" Threw him back in the water, threw him as far as she could. And said, "I'm not drawing any more water out of this well. Out of this—this river."

And so the first daughter said, "Well, you can go back and face our mother if you want to, but I'm not going to. I'm going to do it again." And she put her bucket down, and there was the third Rawhead and Bloodybones. And she said, "Get away from me!" And threw him far over to the other edge of the bank.

They both stormed off, determined they weren't going to take any water back, and they'd had enough of this journey thing, and they weren't going to do it—and headed back toward home.

Well, meanwhile, of course you probably remember that the little old man had wished for their sister good luck—and as *they* walked off from him, he wished for them bad luck. So he didn't have to wish very far, because out of the water, up on the bank crawled the first Rawhead and Bloodybones. And he positioned himself in a place where he could get a little bit of the last bit of daylight coming up. And out of the water crawling up the bank came the second Rawhead and Bloodybones. And he was murky and yucky, but he positioned himself so that he could get a little bit of the last bit of daylight. And the third one did the same thing. He was really grumbling.

And so as the girls walked off in the distance, the first Rawhead and Bloodybones said, "Hmm. They were ugly acting and ugly looking. And so my wish for them is that they would get so ugly, and *be* ugly, that no one would ever want to look at them again. That they would be ugly."

"Ooo—hh," said the second Rawhead and Bloodybones, "that was good. Okay, well, they didn't smell good. They acted ugly, they looked ugly, they didn't smell good, and I wish for them that they would have the worst smell. That they would smell worse than pig-swine, worse than anything that you've ever smelled, and that people would shun them and stay away from them for years and years, because of how bad they smelled."

"Ah, good, good, good," said the others. And the third, who had the longest to crawl, and the most difficult job getting up on the bank, he said, "Well, I wish that when they get to their home, that their heads would feel so heavy they could barely keep their head up. And that when they combed their hair, out from their hair would come snakes and vipers and lizards and toads, and all manner of vermin that would scare and shriek at them. And that they would inhabit all of the land around them."

"Oh, good, good, good," said the others. "Yes."

And so, off went the girls back to their neighboring community. And when they got to the outskirts of town, as their stepsister had done, people did open their windows again and look out, and they were looking, and "*What* is that horrible smell?" And it was so bad that they had to slam down their windows, but they continued to look as the girls went by, and then their eyes just could not bear what they saw. There were these two hideous creatures coming back into town. Oh, my goodness. And as they went, people followed at a very, very faraway distance, just a little bit enough to see where are these hideous, stinky creatures going.

And the same thing happened as they came into town. People ran back into their houses, closed their windows down, and they got to their mother's door, and came up to her yard, and came to her door. And she ran out to meet them, and, "Ooh, girls, you are ugly! Ooh, girls, you do smell bad! Pee-you! But that's okay, we're going to be rich, I can stand you, I can stand being made to be with you. Come on in here. Let me comb your hair."

And so they went, and they said, "Oh, our heads feel so heavy, and we're so tired from the big trip, and we didn't get any water. All we got was stinking old Rawhead and Bloodybones," and complain, complain.

And she said, "Now, it's okay, sweet girls, it's all right. Just sit right down here, and let me comb your hair." And she started to comb. And out of their hair came snakes and vermin of all types and lizards and snails and everything you could imagine that was creepy and crawly and awful to look at. And she *shrieked* and put up her dress and said, "I'm leaving here *forever,* " and off she ran into the night.

Well, the girls were quarreling with each other: "*You* made her do that!" "*You* made her do that!" "No, you!" "No, you!"

Meanwhile, our beautiful, sweet-smelling girl was sitting and looking at her gold and her diamonds and her pearls. And who should ride up just at that moment, to come into the community to stay overnight, but the handsome prince. And when he saw our beautiful, beautiful young woman, and all of these riches, it was a combination too irresistible to leave. And the others girls had gone off fighting anyway, and so of course he fell madly in love with her—how could you not?—and he asked her to be his bride. And he had his men gather up all her riches—I mean, why leave it behind?—and off they went into their own section of the kingdom to live happy ever after.

Carl Lindahl

Sounding a Shy Tradition: Oral and Written Styles of American Mountain Märchen

IN CHARACTERISTIC MÄRCHEN FASHION, this study is thick with threes. I seize upon three localized American storytelling traditions, three literary translators of folktales, and three traits widely held to be definitive of the oral form known as the Märchen. Recovering the performances of the oral storytellers and then weighing their styles, I consider what the discursive space between these tales and their literary counterparts can tell us both about the tellers and their editors: which aspects of oral tradition have been excised or transformed in written versions? What do these changes reveal about scholarly preconceptions regarding folk culture and oral art? Finally, and most importantly, what can we discover about the artistry and values of the mountain Märchen as told in living contexts and on the tellers' own terms?

The three oral traditions and their literary translators are the Hicks-Harmon family of western North Carolina and eastern Tennessee, as portrayed by Richard Chase; the Muncy family of eastern Kentucky, as presented by Leonard Roberts; and the Ozark mountaineers of the Arkansas-Missouri border, as represented by Vance Randolph. These are the regions and writers that have effectively defined the British- and Irish-American folk Märchen as it is broadly understood today.

American folklore *about* our folklore invests enormous importance in the Appalachians and the Ozarks, two regions similarly isolated and mountainous, similarly said to preserve in "pure form" the oldest traditions of the nation's English, Irish, and Scottish ancestry. These two regions have long been credited with harboring archaic folk speech traditions of "Shakespearian" or even Chaucerian English, and they are thought single-handedly to have preserved the oral Märchen.

Although sociolinguists have long debunked the notion that Chaucer or Shakespeare would feel comfortable listening to the everyday speech of mountaineers, the fruits of the past eighty years of folklore fieldwork strongly suggest that the two regions have indeed preserved the lion's share of British- and Irish-American Märchen. Of the fifteen major published collections of British- and Irish-American Märchen, fourteen mine these two regions exclusively, and the ten most influential of these fourteen are the creations of only three men—Richard Chase, Vance Randolph, and Leonard Roberts. Thus, their three voices have spoken disproportionately loudly about the nature of mountain Märchen.[1] We must consider carefully the work of these men just to find a hint of the underlying traditions that they represented, however well or poorly.

I. The Perfect Structure of the Märchen:
The Hicks-Harmon Family and Richard Chase

For those who view folklore as a sort of entertaining subliterature, the Märchen genre—comprising stories known also as "magic" or "fairy" tales—is the pinnacle of traditional oral prose expression, reaching rarified heights so uncharacteristic of folklore that it is seen to occupy that tiny place where literature and folklore overlap. The Märchen, many argue, is one of the few folk forms worthy of that otherwise oxymoronic appellation "oral art." While some literati condescendingly persist in seeing oral Märchen as "the life-lightening trash of pre-literate peoples" (Updike 1981:126), others follow the lead of Francis Lee Utley, who views these tales as small-scale masterpieces whose perfect structure and digestible size make them ideal vehicles for consideration as works of art (1975).

Many before and after Utley also characterize the Märchen as a structure encapsulating a special message that endures regardless of the diction in which it might be clothed. The formalists and the structuralists who dominated folklore studies during much of the twentieth century—as well as the evolutionists and the comparativists who preceded them—characterized the Märchen as a form, an outline, and/or a sequence of events. Major proponents of these and other approaches located the magic of the Märchen in its seeming ability to transcend both the identity of the teller and the language in which it was conveyed. For the great majority of nineteenth- and early twentieth-century folklorists, the structure of the folktale *was*, in effect, its style: to know the pattern of the tale was to know its essence and all that it had to offer. Thus, scholars produced innumerable books and established such monograph series as Folklore Fellows Communications, largely for the purpose of plotting folktale structures and positing their Urforms, Normalforms, and other idealized shapes.

The persistence of stable Märchen plots, recognizable over centuries and across hundreds of cultural contexts, seemed to justify this form-driven approach to the folktale. The name of the heroine might change—Cinderella could as easily be Aschenputtel, All-Furs, Catskins, or Vasilisa—but tellers removed by twelve hundred years or twelve thousand miles can still recognize the ninth-century Chinese story of Sheh Hsien as a version of the tale we most often call Cinderella. Such amazing structural persistence has been ascribed to what Hasan El-Shamy has called "a delicate balance" of the tales' parts, which have been chiseled into an unforgettable form that both aids in their transmission and secures their imperishable values to all who hear them. These perfect structures balance the seeming universality of their appeal against an individual's authorship, or ownership, or power to interpret them.[2]

Thus we find numerous collections of folktales prefaced by pronouncements about the assumed age and anonymity of the Märchen form. Quoting a Breton storyteller, Geneviève Massignon states a view held by many traditional narrators as well as folklorists: that Märchen can seem "so old that no one knows if anyone ever invented them" (Massignon 1965:12). It is as if these tales have made themselves up. If so, their anonymity could be assumed to speak for an entire world, nation, or class. As the Grimms famously stated, *Das Volk dichtet:* the "folk" make poetry; the Märchen, the most poetic of oral prose forms, is the creation of a collectivity rather than the work of a single artist—its art exists independently of the teller. According to such formulations, a ballad may issue, generically, "from the mouth of a milk maid," but a whole, unselfconscious folk has shared in its creation; similarly, any given storyteller is merely the unreflective vehicle of a vast impersonal tradition. Only those who stand outside and above the oral tradition possess sufficient intelligence to determine a tale's meaning.

By depriving individual folk narrators of agency in creating the Märchen, we have simply guaranteed that we will see ourselves in these tales much more clearly than we do their tellers, and thus we take it upon ourselves as individuals to say what a peasant's, a farmer's, or a teacher's Märchen means. This move clears the stage for Bruno Bettelheim or Carl Jung or Robert Bly to seize upon a literary reworking of an oral tale and, never having visited among the communities that shared it as a living performance, to pronounce both precisely and universally what that tale is about.

As early as the beginning of the nineteenth century, literary artists pressured would-be folklorists to "restore" their orally collected materials to imagined perfect forms presumably implicit in, but missing from, the original oral tellings. As the Grimms were beginning to fashion the Märchen into an icon of the folk imagination, they attempted to represent the performances of the tellers more or less accurately. But esthetes were not impressed. After the brothers had shared their attempts at faithful transcription with Clemens Brentano, a celebrated romantic poet and one of their idols, Brentano wrote, "If you want to display children's clothing, you can do that quite well without bringing out an outfit that has buttons torn off it, dirt smeared on it, and the shirt hanging out of the pants." Why, his appalled response suggested, do you represent the torn remnants of these tales when it is in your power to tell them as they should be told? (Tatar 1987:16)

The Grimms took Brentano's advice. The template that would generate one of the world's most published books—as well as hundreds of imitative folktale collections from "folk cultures" worldwide— was shaped by this correspondence. For example, regardless of what the Norwegians Asbjornsen and Moe or the Russian Afanasyev may have *heard* performed as oral tradition, the tales they published strikingly resembled those in the Grimms' book. Following Brentano's argumentation and Wilhelm Grimm's new practice, each "collector" became a self-appointed "corrector" and in the process the sole author and explicator of the folktale. The corrector proclaimed, in effect, "These tales come from and belong to everyone, but it is only I who can show you their true form and what they mean."

Let us follow the ideas of a perfect form and the need for a perfect interpreter into the Appalachians. Richard Chase, by far the best known and most influential of the three major American collectors, stumbled upon a far-flung family tradition (sometimes known as the Harmon-Hicks-Ward-Gentry-Long tradition, but here identified more tersely as Hicks-Harmon). Numerous family members—who had never met each other—were so reverent of the received forms of their tales that they preserved the identical sequence of actions in the great majority of their tellings. If any one group of American tales can present a case for testing the idea of the presumed identity of the Märchen's form and message, the Hicks-Harmon family repertoire can.

W. F. H. Nicolaisen identifies David Hicks Sr. as the probable bearer of these tales to the New World, a claim supported by the current oral tradition of the Hicks-Harmon family, who insist that their Märchen repertoire derives from England (1994:126). When David Hicks left England, about 1760, chapbook tales recounting the exploits of a boy named Jack were circulating; these and oral versions provided entertainment for a huge and varied audience, both literate and nonliterate. "Jack the Giant Killer"—first known to be printed in 1711 as "The History of Jack and the Giants"—was repeatedly published in cheap portable editions. Jack and his exploits attracted attention and commentary from such literary giants as Henry Fielding and Samuel Johnson (Opie and Opie 1974:50).

When David Hicks arrived in America, the mountains were already filled with Märchen, as attested by Joseph Doddridge, who described the narrative pastimes of the West Virginia frontier when he was a boy in the 1760s: "Dramatic narrations, chiefly concerning Jack and the Giant, furnished our young people with another source of amusement during their leisure hours" (in Perdue 1987:97). In Doddridge's recollections, the structure of the stories assumed an importance equal to that of their content: "Many of those tales were lengthy, and embraced a considerable range of incident. Jack, always the hero of the story, after encountering many difficulties and performing many great achievements, came off conqueror of the Giant. These dramatic narrations . . . were so arranged as to the different incidents of the narration, that they were easily committed to memory"(97). Note the attention paid to the tales' perfectly memorable form. Doddridge went on to state that these tales had already been swept away by "civilization," which had "substituted in their place the novel and the romance." But the Jack tales continued to be told among mountain people, a fact that folklorists did not rediscover until the 1920s, more than a century and a half after Doddridge heard them, when Isabel Gordon Carter asked a celebrated ballad singer if she knew any folktales.

The singer was Jane Gentry, of Hot Springs, North Carolina. She knew a dozen long narratives often told in her family, which she identified by the name "Old Jack, Will, and Tom Tales." But she expressed utter astonishment that any outsider would want to know these stories (Carter 1925:340). Apparently, these tales weren't for everybody: they were intimate and personal, told often and with animation within the group, most often to keep children working (Ellis 1994; Lindahl 1994a).

Something had slowly but clearly happened between 1765 and 1923: what had been a popular and public art form spanning the range of social classes and situations was now (at least in the context of the Hicks-Harmon family tradition) a *working-class* act, inextricably associated with the hard luck and labor of the mountain poor. This was a private, stay-at-home art form that, no matter how lively inside its native boundaries, was quite shy and elusive to the outsider.

The mountain Märchen emerged from hiding in 1943, when Richard Chase published *The Jack Tales,* easily the most popular collection of American folktales ever compiled—and still in print today. Tapping the same family to which Jane Gentry belonged—the Hicks-Harmon family of North Carolina—Chase produced a book so influential that it helped perpetuate two substantial fallacies: that American Märchen were pretty much the legacy of one family and that the characteristic tales were about a boy named Jack (Lindahl 1994a:xxii-xxvii).

Unlike the universalist folklorists who then dominated early Märchen scholarship, Chase at least assigned names and a family pedigree to the tradition behind his tales, but his *modus operandi* imitated that employed by the Grimms more than a century before. He too conflated the stories of as many as ten different tellers into one Normalform rendered in his own words, thus subordinating the diverse artful voices of his sources to his personal aesthetic. The working contexts and the local references that made these tales so much the special province of the Appalachians are obscured in his versions.

The various ways in which Chase changed his sources are discussed elsewhere in this volume; most important for the discussion at hand is the fact that Chase saw his *Jack Tales* as a coherent cycle reflecting the personality of the protagonist Jack, a figure who stood as "the unassuming representative of a very large part of the American people" (1943:xii). The ideal shape of Chase's mountain Märchen thus served largely as a vehicle to express the personality of an ideal character, Jack. Although some authors have followed Chase's lead in finding the southern Appalachian Jack to be a consistent figure (Carrière 1946; Gutierrez 1978), others, in comparing tales from British, Irish, and North American communities, have seen in "Jack" little more than an all-purpose name, which any given narrator or family tradition may choose to invest with a distinct personality (Nicolaisen 1978; Lindahl 1994a). Chase's Jack is often so different from the various Jacks presented by mountain storytellers that it could be argued that Chase invented a pseudo-oral literary genre in *The Jack Tales* just as the Grimms had invented the dominant form of the literary Märchen, and that Chase's book—like the Grimm brothers' collection—strongly influenced subsequent published folktale collections as well as oral performances.

Today, certain members of the Hicks-Harmon family, including Ray Hicks and Frank Proffitt Jr., do see Jack as a fully developed being, a character so vivid that he can almost come to life; when telling their tales, they see themselves as Jack (Lindahl 1994b; McDermitt 1983). Yet certain family members, again including Ray Hicks, have gone on record as disapproving of Chase's treatments of the Hicks-Harmon oral tradition (Woestendiek 1990). As Chase's book has significantly influenced at least some of the recorded oral performances of some members of the family,[3] it is of fundamental importance to note that one family member has left us recorded performances that predate Chase's book, offering us considerable insight into aspects of the Hicks-Harmon narrative tradition as it existed before Chase attempted to redefine it. These tellings present a central character significantly different from Chase's Jack.

The teller is Samuel Harmon, great-great uncle of today's most celebrated Jack tale teller, Ray Hicks. Samuel was the grandson of Council Harmon, to whom Chase attributed the oral Jack tale tradition, but also, on his mother's side, the grandson of Samuel ("Little Sammy") Hicks II. It was from "Granddaddy Hicks" that Harmon learned his folktales. During a lengthy collecting expedition for the

Archive of American Folk Song and the Works Progress Administration in April 1939, Herbert Halpert visited Samuel Harmon, who was then living with his son Austin near Maryville, Tennessee, in the Great Smoky Mountains. Accompanying Halpert was Mellinger E. Henry, who had published a number of the family's songs in *Folk Songs of the Southern Highlands* (1938). The primary intent of the visit was to record songs and instrumental performances, but during a second visit, twenty-five days after Halpert had first met the Harmons, Sam began to tell him tales.

Halpert, acutely aware of the importance of context in the transmission and collection of folklore, asked Sam how he'd learned and told his stories. Sam described learning his tales from his grandfather and telling them in turn to his grandchildren, who would beg him so insistently for stories that he sometimes had to make them up in order to meet their demands:

> Herbert Halpert: How did you come . . . to make up your own stories?
> Samuel Harmon: Why, I told all I knowed and then I had to go to make em up myself and telling em. We—
> HH: Did they used to pester you, bother you to tell stories?
> SH: Yeah. I stayed with my son and he had a house dug in the ground and through the summertime, why, me and the kids would lay in that house down in the ground there—it's called a storm house. And they just weared the life out of me to tell em tales. And I told em tales and tales and tales and told em all I did know and then I just had to go to making em up some and telling em to get shet of em, to get rid of em. "Why," they'd say, "Grandpa, *do* tell us another tale. Grandpa, do *please* tell us one more tale and we'll let you alone." Well, I'd get so sleepy that it appeared to me like I just couldn't keep my eyes open. And I'd tell em one. . . . (AFS 2929A2)

Halpert's fieldnotes include the observation that most of the family songs recorded during his visit with the Harmons indeed followed a grandparent-grandchild line of transmission, in which the oldest members of the household would entertain and teach the youngest (Halpert 1939:47). Because Sam Harmon's storytelling grandfather died when Sam was about ten years old, Sam's tales were children's stories in two senses: they arose from his own childhood memories as he passed them on to an audience of children very nearly the same age that he had been when he heard them from his grandfather. In one of the Halpert 1939 recordings, Sam and his granddaughter

Alberta, age eleven, give voice to the special bond between the oldest and youngest as they perform, together, a version of the Cinderella tale "Catskins" (AFS 2916A2–2927A1). Given the way in which Harmon associated his tales so strongly with his own vanished childhood and considering that small children were his primary audience, it seems reasonable to examine the possibility that he would identify both himself and his grandchildren, at least to some extent, with the boy-hero Jack.

Among Halpert's notes there is one brief reference to Sam's feelings about Jack: "Mr. Harmon said humorously: 'If I'd a knowed it in time, I'd a named all of my boys Jack. I never knowed a Jack but what was lucky'" (Halpert 1939:60). This observation is particularly telling in light of the fact that, even to the present day, members of the Hicks-Harmon family in the Beech Mountain area of North Carolina (where Sam Harmon's father was born) still refer to their folktale hero as "Lucky Jack" (Gutierrez 1978: 86–90, 106).

Beyond this brief reference, only the testimony of Sam Harmon's narrative performances survives to tell us how he felt about Jack. But these performances speak deeply. When Harmon's version of one tale is set alongside Chase's literary creation, two significantly different heroes come to life, and Chase's "unassuming" Jack emerges as a good deal less humble than he would have us believe. Listening to Sam Harmon tell "Stiff Dick" while reading "Jack and the Varmints," the cognate tale published by Chase, we discover much about the delicate balance of Märchen structure and, for all its perfection, how little it has to do with communicating an invariable meaning (see Chase 1943:58–66). The difference between the two men's titles suggests major divergences in the two tellers' intent and meaning, even as their greatly different performances maintain an almost identical shape.

What the Märchen shape *does*—beyond aiding the memory of listener and teller—is a crucial question to keep before us as we compare the two tales and continue to raise more specific questions of meaning. If the Märchen does indeed enfold a consistent message within its perfect form, that message is most likely connected with the concept of justice. I once asked a French Canadian narrator why he persisted telling the magic tales that so much of the world considers worthy only of children; he answered, "There has to be one place in the world where everything turns out the way it should." It is fair to say that, for the tellers I've known best, the Märchen is about justice if it is about anything, and it ends justly more surely than it ends happily.

Märchen justice is of a peculiar type. As often as not, there is no human agent for this justice; sometimes there is not even a personified supernatural agent. Unlike the typical Western of the 1930s–1950s—in which a hyperjust hero, like Gary Cooper or Alan Ladd or Roy Rogers, effects a just outcome through sheer moral courage—justice often *simply happens* in the American Märchen. It is less the job of the hero than of the plot. Story structure is in many ways simply an externalization of the inner rewards of virtue. The hero's riches come as a reward for simply being who she or he is—when no one else is watching.

Yet, looking more closely at the American mountain Märchen, we find that their heroes often possess—if nothing else—just a shred of verbal agency: a power to rename the situations in which they find themselves. In Sam Harmon's "Stiff Dick," Jack is walking down the road when he sees seven large green flies sitting on a pile "where that cat had been" and swats them all dead with a paddle. Down the road he finds a blacksmith who makes him a belt buckle inscribed with the legend:

Stiff Dick
Killed Seven at a Lick.

Jack's belt buckle then attracts the attention of the king. By re-naming a simple act, Jack is elevated to significant social power, but he is also exposed to danger. The king retains Jack to rid his woods of a unicorn, a boar, and a lion. In each case, the king offers half the money up front, Jack attempts to leave the woods with half the money by avoiding the monster altogether, the beast comes upon Jack as he is attempting his escape and then traps itself as Jack is attempting to flee from it. The first beast is a unicorn that charges Jack, horn down, and—as Jack dodges—literally runs *into* a tree, impaling itself on the trunk. Jack walks back to the king's house and tells the king where he can find the unicorn if he wants to kill it, and then collects the other half of the reward money. In his next adventure, Jack again takes the money and is escaping through the woods when the boar chases him into an abandoned cabin. Jack climbs the wall and waits for the boar to go to sleep, then leaves the cabin, closing the door on the beast;

once more, he returns to the king, tells where the animal is trapped, and receives the other half of the promised money.

On the third day, Jack is offered another $1000 for a third beast; this is how Sam Harmon finishes his tale:

> The lion was yet to get. He [Jack] just knowed in his own mind that he'd get around that lion and not find it out. He started and traveled on and begin to think he's out of reach of the lion, [but] about between sundown and dark the lion found him out.
>
> Here they come. Jack, he run up a tree. And the lion, he went to gnawing the tree. He gnawed the tree and gnawed, kept gnawing—had the tree until it was weaving backwards and forwards. Just about daylight, the old lion got so tired and sleepy and he just laid down beneath the tree and went to sleep.
>
> And Jack thought: now whiles he's asleep, he'd ease down and get away while the lion is asleep. . . . There's a dead limb on the tree about ten foot above the lion and he got down and went to get down that dead limb to peep over, to see . . . the lion's eyes—he was well, good asleep.
>
> He stepped on that limb. And the limb broke and fell right astraddle the lion and he wound his hands in this wood and went to hollering and screaming as hard as he could scream and got the lion excited and the lion went . . . just as hard as he could fly through the woods.
>
> And he happened to run right through the king's yard. And the king demanded to run out and shoot him quick. And they run out and shot the lion. And Jack said, "Now," he said, "you have to pay me another thousand dollars." Says, "I'm just a breaking this lion," said, "for the king's riding horse."

At this precise moment Sam Harmon's tale ends—unlike Chase's literary spinoff or other typical published tales, which carry "happily ever after" codas. Sam Harmon's Jack has the last word in his tale: at the end (with the words "king's riding horse") as in the beginning (with the rhyme on his belt), Jack is elevated by his power to rename a situation, winning with words what he cannot capture any other way. To a greater extent than Chase's, Sam Harmon's tale emphasizes Jack's resourcefulness. Jack's words are stronger than his legs. Though he cannot outrun these beasts, his verbal characterizations capture them and the king's reward as well. The tale and the tale's protagonist present us ways of "winning with words" when all else is lost.

Again, Harmon's tale and Chase's would appear identical, or very nearly so, if presented in outline form—and if the style of the Märchen were its structure, we would have here two undifferentiated versions of the same thing. Yet seemingly small stylistic differences make these two entirely different tales. Sam Harmon saves and weighs his words; Chase bastes the same plot with wordfat; one gets the sense that neither Chase nor his hero will ever stop talking.[4] But beyond this contrast between economy and waste, there are two other substantial differences that inflect the meanings we derive from the Märchen structures: 1) character motivation and 2) the closely related question of just who an "American" Märchen hero is supposed to be.

Consider the two men's characterizations of Jack. In Chase's published version, he is introduced with these words:

> Jack was a-goin' about over the country one time, happened he passed by a place where a man had been rivin' boards, saw a little thin piece and picked it up, started in to whittlin' on it. Jack was so lazy he never noticed much what he was doin' till he'd done made him a little paddle. (Chase 1943:58)

Compare Sam Harmon's opening:

> One time this orphan boy raised up, he just made what he made out of hisself. His mother wasn't much, and he had no father and he just roved here and yonder everywhere till he got—he got to be a young man.

Poverty, no issue for Chase, becomes *the* issue for Sam Harmon, and it fuels the machinery of Märchen justice by giving Jack a need to succeed. Harmon's boy is poor but determined to survive; Chase's is simply lazy and flip (a thematic contrast between economy and waste, to complement the stylistic contrast of these same two qualities).

The focal drama of Sam Harmon's tale lies in the tension between poverty and fear. Harmon's Jack needs the money and would not try to escape without it. This is how Harmon portrays Jack's response to his first reward from the king:

> [The king paid Jack] five hundred dollars, just pleased the poor boy to death, you know—he never did have no money, and he thinks now he'll slip around and get out of there and not run across him [the boar].

Chase's Jack, on the other hand, has no poverty to motivate him; and though fear is part of his experience, even fear is subordinated to Jack's rationality:

> Jack he knowed that if the King was so scared of that hog, it must be awful dangerous. Decided he'd just not get mixed up with such a varmint. (Chase 1943:59–60)

Chase's Jack acts with both reason and swagger. Chase's boy, as I see him, is a study in undermotivated cleverness and bears an uncanny resemblance to Chase himself: he saunters through the landscape and takes what he wants from it, knowing that whatever the cost to others, he will ultimately be rewarded for his caginess. Sam Harmon's Jack, by contrast, is caught in a vise between need and fear and can work his way out of it only by relying on one thing that no one else possesses: his own words. The Märchen is indeed the place where everything turns out the way it should; for the teller and for us it is equally adaptable to both perspectives.

The poor, fearful, but resourceful boy that Sam Harmon presents was no fantasy in Harmon's day and place. Appalachian culture has long been characterized as the property of poor but largely self-sufficient agrarians who farmed their own land. But the cultural reality was significantly different. More than 40 percent of the Appalachian families of the nineteenth century did not own their own land; they wandered through the mountain landscape, much as Harmon's Jack does, with great needs and greater hopes, working other people's land, often bound as indentured servants to landlords, whose tyrannical rule is represented in such barely fictionalized roles as that of the king in "Stiff Dick" (Dunaway 1996:51–122). No more than 10 percent of Jack's flesh-and-blood Appalachian alter egos ever reached the self-sufficiency of land ownership or other forms of material independence, but Harmon's Jack was one of many who spoke for the aspirations of the struggling nine-tenths who, when they could win no other way, won through the justice of the Märchen. The Hicks-Harmon family, sometimes idealized as totally self-sufficient and planted permanently on the slopes of Beech Mountain, may indeed have been more settled and land rich than the wandering heroes depicted in their tales. But even when planted on their own land, family members engaged in migratory work and often—like their hero Jack—relied upon their traveling labors to provide them a thin margin of material comfort (Isbell 1996). Furthermore, some family members, like Sam's father and Sam himself, wandered off Beech Mountain to find their lands and modest livings on other slopes, in other states. For some, the wandering persisted almost to the end. As old men who could no longer support themselves on their own homesteads, both Little Sammy Hicks and his grandson Sam Harmon traveled to move in with their sons (Halpert 1939:47). Thus, it was from the aged traveler, Little Sammy, that Sam Harmon first heard his Jack tales, and Sam himself had to leave his home to travel to the farm in Tennessee where he taught the same tales to his grandchildren.

Chase's Jack, however, like most of the Jacks that appear in published collections, no longer speaks for the disenfranchised tellers. Chase simply ignores their poverty and silences the strategies with which they pursue their dreams. The justice of the Märchen is highly specific and easily suppressed as tales pass from speech to print, and one of the great failures of American folklore scholarship is to mistake the skeleton of justice for the real thing by ignoring the intensely local and personal ethos that these tales convey for their native speakers. The perfect structure of the Märchen is one of perfect flexibility; presented by Samuel Harmon or Richard Chase, Jack becomes, by turns, the mirror-like agent of each teller and interpreter. At least as I read them, "Stiff Dick" and "Jack and the Varmints" are irreconcilably different tales.

II. The Brilliant Images of Märchen: The Muncy Family and Leonard Roberts

I now turn to a second salient Märchen trait as identified by folklorists, on the one hand, and employed by mountain storytellers, on the other. As closely identified with the Märchen as its imperishable structure is its intense imagery. Max Lüthi, the most incisive analyst of the literary fairy tale, has noted that Märchen imagery tends to be quite sparse but exceedingly—even violently—sharp, offering up brilliant partial pictures that brand themselves on listeners' memories. This imagistic vividness is so intense that it has led Lüthi to speak of "the shock effect of beauty" (Lüthi 1986:1–39). A case in point is the famous Grimm version of "Snow White," which opens

> When the snowflakes were falling like feathers from the sky, a queen was sitting and sewing at a window with a black ebony frame. And as she was sewing and looking out the window, she pricked her finger with the needle, and three drops of blood fell on the snow. The red looked so beautiful on the white snow that she thought to herself, if only I had a child as white as snow, as red as blood, and as black as the wood of the window frame. (Grimm and Grimm 1987:196)

Brilliant as these images are, they pale in comparison to those emerging from less romanticized versions of the same motif. At least six centuries before the Grimm version, the Irish prose tale of "The Exile of the Sons of Uisliu" uses the same imagistic constellation with considerably greater shock effect. The heroine Deirdre watches as a man is flaying a calf in the winter snow. As the red blood splatters on the snow-covered ground, a raven alights to drink the blood. Deirdre stares at this scene of violence and color and proclaims: "I could love a man with those three colours" (Gantz 1981:260).

The Appalachian oral Märchen does indeed present stark and violent imagery and, like its European counterparts, it carries a shock effect. Yet, in contrast to these two European scenes, the Appalachian shock effect is seldom one of beauty. Consider the opening of "Old Greasybeard," as told by Jane Muncy of Hyden, Kentucky, to folklorist Leonard Roberts in 1955 (Roberts 1969). Seventeen-year-old Jane Muncy was Roberts's star narrator.

After Chase, Roberts is the most celebrated editor of Märchen from Appalachia. Unlike Chase, he was a native of the region and he strove to represent the tellers as best he could. Nor did Roberts attempt to cover his tracks; rather, he has left the nation's largest collection of recorded Märchen to Berea College (Roberts 1949–1980). Thus, what I present here represents the most faithful written renderings of oral style to be found among the major collections of mountain Märchen.

In Jane's narration, Tom and Jack and Merrywise have left their starving parents—who can no longer provide for them—to clear some land and fend for themselves. Each day as two of the boys work, a third stays home to cook for the others. The first day's cooking falls to Tom. As he prepared the food

> [a]n old man stuck his head in the door with a great big ten-gallon hat on his head. When he first stuck his head in the door Tom noticed that he had a great big long greasy beard and that his hat looked greasy too. (Roberts 1969:53)

The source of the grease soon becomes apparent. Tom invites the old man to share in the meal, but Greasybeard declines, diverts Tom's attention, and then tosses the entire meal into his giant hat; he sets the hat back on his head and runs off with it. As Jack minds the house the second day, the same thing happens. The third day is Merrywise's turn, and the young boy lays a trap:

Merrywise . . . went out and split a great big log, and he put a wedge in this log to hold it open. . . . In come the old man with his great big long greasy beard. . . .

Merrywise said, "Well come out here, old man. I want to show you something. . . . Look over there on the other side of that big log, old man." So the old man looked over on the other side of the log and his beard hung down into the log that was wedged open and just as his beard got in there good, why Merrywise kicked the wedge out and the log snapped shut. . . . And the old man pulled and pulled and pulled and finally got away. About that time it began to snow and snow and snow and the boys came home. . . . The brothers said, "Let's track him down." . . . The snow made it easy for them and they went outside and they saw his blood and pieces of his old greasy beard laying in the snow and they followed it and followed it and followed it. . . . (Roberts 1969:56–57)

Jane's style betrays how young she is: even a reader can sense her age by noting how often and exactly she repeats the formulaic tags—"old man," "great big long greasy beard"—that help her hold the story together. Yet Jane is an astonishingly accomplished adolescent narrator. It did not surprise me in the least when, after finally locating her two aunts, they told me that Jane had succeeded her grandmother as the family's master storyteller and that, at age fifty-nine, she continued to be a great one.

Comparing young Jane Muncy's performance to the Grimms' "Snow White," we find that the blood on the snow remains a constant, but there is no intimation of beauty in Jane's version. Only very rarely is the physical beauty of a mountain Märchen figure noted and, even then, the violent imagery of beauty is seldom applied to grace that figure. But the violence of human body parts remains an intimate part of the tradition. In one tale told by North Carolinian Lee Wallins, the boy-hero Little Nippy is captured by a giant and his wife (Glassie 1964). The giant asks the boy how he should be punished for stealing from the giant and causing him to kill his children. Nippy replies, "I'd fatten me up and eat me." So indeed Nippy is overfed until, in Nippy's words, "I'm so fat I'll spoil on your hands." Nippy tells the giant that he should go and summon his neighbors to help with the feast so that no meat would be left to spoil. While the giant is gone, his wife prepares to cut off Nippy's head, but he dodges with his neck and the wife keeps missing him. Nippy tells the woman that she can't see well enough to cut off his head because "You've got pie

crustes in your eyes" (a mountain reference to the mucus that collects in the eyes of sleepers and that many Americans euphemistically
label "sleep in the eyes"). He offers to assist the old woman by remov-
ing the "pie crustes," but as she lies down to accept his help he cuts
off her head and throws it into the boiling cauldron that was to serve
as Nippy's cooking pot. The old giant returns home and awaits the
feast, but begins to smell something burning in the pot. He sings out,
"Old woman, old woman, your meat's a-burnin' up," and finally goes
to the pot to see his wife's long blond hair waving in the boiling water
(Glassie 1964:97). This is the only physical description of a character
to be found in this lengthy tale—and, again, the teller presents us
with an unforgettable image of physical terror, not beauty.

Returning to the rich family storytelling tradition of Jane Muncy's
grandmother and aunts, we find that every tale is likely to contain
two or three arresting, violently sharp images that impress themselves
on the memories of tellers and listeners alike. In one tale, the signal
image is an "overgrown toe" that a hungry man finds in a potato patch;
he cooks it and eats it, and that night its spectral owner comes back
to reclaim it by eating the man and his dogs. This tale, known in the
family as "Old Overgrown Toe," is named for its ruling image. In
another Muncy family tale, the title again recalls the story's dominant image: "Rawhead and Bloodybones" (Roberts 1955:54–58). Here,
a mistreated stepdaughter is sent on a long mission to recover water
from a distant well that is guarded by several amorphous figures named
Rawhead and Bloodybones. When the girl reaches the water each
monstrous blob chants to her, "Wash me off and dry me off and turn
me over easy." She does this and, returning home, finds that her scalp
is itching. When she runs a comb through her hair, gold spills onto
her lap (a rare instance of imagistic beauty found in the Appalachian
Märchen).[5]

In discussions with four members of the tale-rich Muncy family, I
found that only one—besides, of course, Jane herself—remembered
many tales, and only one other would retell at least a few tales coher-
ently and with style. This narrator, Glen Muncy Anderson, did not
consider herself a storyteller and would not even compare herself to
her grandmother (Rachel Farmer), her mother (Sidney Farmer
Muncy), her sister (Hope), or her niece (Jane). But all family members—whether or not they felt confident retelling the tales in detail—
retained the salient images of "Rawhead and Bloodybones" and the

"Old Overgrown Toe" indelibly in their minds. These images are sparingly described but vividly retained as mental pictures, fuller and often more frightening than the words used to describe them. Thus
Glen Muncy Anderson recalls both the image of Rawhead and
Bloodybones and the terror that she felt when, as a child of four, she
would listen to her mother tell this tale:

> It would scare me to death. I was four; it was total dark and I'd be in bed
> in the corner, with my two brothers in other beds and my mother in the
> big bed, all in the same room. The boys would clamor and clamor to
> hear "Rawhead and Bloodybones"—and I'd think, "Oh, no, here we go
> again. Scare me to death." I'd be awake all night. . . .
>
> Do you see how that might scare a little four-year-old girl sleeping off
> in the corner by herself? . . . I could picture just a bloody mass of bones,
> and it would scare me bad. (Anderson and Muncy 1997)

This tale and "Old Overgrown Toe" were stories that Mrs. Anderson can relate with considerable art, seventy years after hearing her
mother tell them. But there are several others that she now remembers only as images. The story of "Bully Bornes" (a version of which is
told by Jane in Roberts 1955:60–63), for example, she recalls only as
a single image, pictured through the eyes of the heroine, who is vic-
timized by her monstrous husband, the prizefighter Bully Bornes.

> I remember Bully Bornes being so mean to her. And she would go up in
> the tall attic, way up on top of the house, and would look down and see
> him coming. I don't remember too much about that. It's been a long,
> long time ago.
>
> But I can still see that girl looking out the window as she hears the
> ground shake, looking at the terrible man come thundering at her up
> the road. (Anderson and Muncy 1997)

The power with which Märchen images impress visual memories upon
their listeners should lead us to question the idea that these tales
survive solely because of their perfectly memorable structures. There
is substantial evidence to the contrary. Rather than memorizing plots,
tellers "see" their stories in their minds' eyes, hanging their memories of the tale on one or more spectacular images.

Muncy family members, like most of the mountain families who
maintained Märchen traditions well into recent memory, were not
estranged from the hardships suffered by their folktale protagonists—
the starving man who eats the overgrown toe or the other country
folk who people their tales. The Muncys were a family of teachers

and farmers, plying both traditions to make ends meet and traveling widely, like the folktale protagonist Jack, in a seasonal rhythm from farm to town. As the coal industry was redefining the Kentucky mountain economy, Jane Muncy's grandfather left both of his modest but sufficient jobs and led the family on a walk across two counties to a new home near his workplace as a carpenter in the mines of Perry County. Within a few years, during the Great Depression, grandfather Willman Muncy died from injuries sustained in the coal mines, and the family was exposed to greater need than it had known before. Willman's widow, Sidney Farmer Muncy, the great storyteller who fed the family tradition, began running a boarding house to help sustain the family. The Muncy tales are realistic reflections of a difficult farm life, seasoned by more recent memories of an even more difficult life in a perilous and ultimately too-costly profession. The grit of the imagery and the tales' intimations of poverty underline that tough life. Again, literary editors have been unkind to the mountain Märchen: they have tried continually to smooth the grit out of these tales and, in so doing, compromised the stories' power.

If we learn much from pathology about what constitutes health, we may learn more about how and why tales are remembered from narrative failure than from narrative success. One of the great strengths of Leonard Roberts's work was that he collected hundreds of tales that he never published. These half-remembered tales document indisputably that passive bearers—as well as many of the active tellers of the mountain Märchen—remember the story not as a memorized plot but as a succession of unforgettable images. Roberts is the only one of the three major collectors of British-American Märchen who documented this tradition principally with voice recordings that have survived, allowing the testimony of the tellers to show how powerfully the imagery worked in the development and continuance of this tradition (Roberts 1949–1980).

The tales told by reluctant narrators present significant evidence for the important role of internally visualized images in the process of recreating tales. Glen Muncy Anderson had been so terrified by such images as Rawhead and Bloodybones that she refused to retell her mother's tales to her own children. Glen's niece Jane, however, deeply enjoyed the stories, listened to them not just willingly but lovingly, and nourished them as family treasures that she passed on in performances to her children and grandchildren. When I finally had the opportunity to meet and listen to Jane, then aged sixty-two, she affirmed that she indeed retained powerful mental images of her grandmother's folktales, but these images did not impede her love of the stories:

> I didn't find the Rawhead and Bloodybones scary at all. I thought of them as benevolent, even though I could picture them: I pictured them as a skull, with bones underneath them like crosses, sort of like the kind you might see on a poison medicine bottle—with some bloody, gory stuff coming on them, but they were so good to this good—to the heroine that, that they had to be pretty good critters. And I think that, I think that's true, no matter what it looks like, or how you describe it, if it's good on the inside, it's good. If it does good, it's good. (Fugate 2000)

Jane's memories—no less powerful than her aunt Glen's—were tempered by her sense of the creatures' benevolent role in the story as a whole. In June of 2000, I listened to Jane tell intricate and beautifully crafted versions of her grandmother's stories and heard her comment at length upon her personal process of storytelling. "I think in pictures very vividly," she told me; as Jane's grandmother told her tales, "*my* picture from my head . . . my pictures were filling in all the details that she didn't tell me." By visualizing the unsaid implications of her grandmother's words, Jane held the stories together pictorially. Jane's storytelling teacher, Sidney Farmer Muncy, was rare in the amount of detail she invested in her Märchen. She was, in Jane's words, "a detail person" as well as an artist in many media, including drawing and poetry. As a teacher and devoted reader, she also cultivated a sense of the importance of the written word which she passed on to her entire family. It is then especially important to note that, even with the powerful literary influences that Grandmother Sidney exerted upon the family, Jane remembered her tales more vividly as pictures than as words and used varying words at each telling to retranslate her strong visual impressions into verbal form. Her mental image of Rawhead and Bloodybones helps her remember the story, yet in her recent retelling she does not describe the creature, but simply calls it "a funny-looking thing," leaving her listeners to create mental images of their own, just as she had done listening to Sidney Farmer Muncy's tales half a century before.

In discussing the ways in which she visualizes "Merrywise," her favorite among the tales learned from her grandmother, Jane once again affirmed how she fashioned words from internalized pictures. Now, as a grandmother, Jane invests many more words in telling "Merrywise" than she did as an eleven-year-old in 1949 (when Roberts recorded her telling the same tale), but the images remain stark and relatively unexplained. In both the 1949 recording and in Jane's performance of June 2000, the one character described at any length is the witch.

But as Jane retells the tales, she *sees* much more than she tells. For example, she retains a powerfully visualized sense of the appearance of the central character, Merrywise:

> He was small, smaller than the other boys of course, maybe up to their shoulders. And he wore sort of a knickers kind of clothing, like little boys would wear. He had a little boy haircut that maybe came down over his ears. It was sort of round, and he had freckles. I had freckles too. [My grandmother] always told me that *she* had freckles as a child. . . . And freckles made you beautiful. And if you had freckles you would stay much younger than the other people your age. I didn't want to be younger than my age, and I didn't particularly want to have their freckles that matched my pigtail, but she told me about her freckles. . . . She said, "You know, when I was a little girl, I didn't like my freckles either." And so, when I pictured Merrywise, I pictured Merrywise as sandy blond hair and freckles—sort of like me. *Surprise. Surprise.* (Fugate 2000)

In spite of the fact that Jane sees Merrywise so vividly as she recalls and tells his story, she does not expend one word on describing the boy within the tale itself.

Although Jane Muncy's current versions of her grandmother's tales are often at least twice and sometimes more than three times the length of the tales she told to Leonard Roberts half a century ago, she remains true to the principle of letting the most powerful images speak for themselves. Yet in continuing to tell the tales, Jane shares one of the concerns that led her aunt Glen to refrain from telling them at all: both narrators worried about the potential of these images to frighten their children. Jane explains:

> Well, in the story, as I told it to my children and my grandchildren, . . . because they're not going to hear it as often as I did . . . I want them to get the moral, and I want them to see what the value is. And they can be a little scared, but I don't want them to focus on the scary parts.

[My grandmother] and her generation, it was okay about the scary parts. That was all right. And you didn't think, "Don't tell a child a scary story."

So in her contemporary tellings, Jane allows the images to speak for themselves even as she crafts long verbal messages to guide her young listeners safely through the potential terrors presented by those images.

The extraordinary, hidden, visual lives of Jane's tales, seen but untold by her, are similar to those that guide storytellers in other parts of the world. Both Vivian Labrie, working with French-Canadian narrators (1979, 1981), and Donald Archie MacDonald, working with Gaelic-speaking storytellers in Scotland (1978), have found that exceptional oral artists in these traditions *see* their stories and recreate them at each telling with verbalizations based on the mental pictures that hold the stories powerfully in their memories.[6]

III. The Unabashed Artistry of the Märchen: Ozark Narrators and Vance Randolph

Finally, and most briefly, a third teller, collector, and trait of the mountain Märchen. Folklorists describe the Märchen as an undisguised fantasy, a mode of expression so uncompromisingly magical that it cannot hide its escapist and fanciful nature. As soon as we hear "Once upon a time"—or, far more often in the American mountains, "One time"—teller and tale have opened up a preserve for pure show, where the verbal art of the teller and the magic of the tale prevail, with no refuge in which they can conceal their arts. Märchen are thus considered by many to be one of the primary folkloric examples of art for art's sake.

If such an uncompromisingly artful context is indeed characteristic of the Märchen, it is bound to clash with Appalachian and Ozark folk cultural aesthetics, which are powerfully utilitarian in nature. In lectures at Indiana University, Henry Glassie has called attention to the magnificently intricate baskets created by mountaineers. Just as remarkable as the dizzying geometric patterns woven by their makers is the fact that the makers themselves tend not to acknowledge their beauty. To express his pride in his creation, one of the great mountain basket makers will take his basket, set it upside-down on his porch, and then jump up and down on it—leaving it surprisingly undamaged—to illustrate how durable it is. Although the maker stresses only his utilitarian skills and refuses to acknowledge his art, his creation is, in Glassie's words, "unnecessarily beautiful."

Thus there exists in the American mountains a strong tendency to call attention away from one's art. How does such an aesthetic treat the Märchen, a verbal site where art presumably cannot hide? One response to this tension is simply not to tell the Märchen; I believe that the clash between Märchen and mountain aesthetics is one of the reasons why the Märchen has been recorded so seldom in the United States. Wishing to tell a magical narrative, but shying away from Märchen, an Appalachian teller may present a tall tale instead— a form in which verbal art is not represented entirely for its own sake, but to perpetrate a practical joke on the listener. Insisting on the truth, the relevance, and the physical proximity of the unbelievable events he narrates (for tall tale tellers tend to be male), the narrator unfolds a string of increasingly incredible accounts as a test of the gullibility of the listener. The art in telling the tall tale lies in calling attention away from the art, in insisting that the story is true. A tall tale teller who laughs at his creation, or lets on that his story might not be true, has broken the rules. He is too admittedly artful to be accepted as a mountain oral artist.

Another strategy for creating verbal art without acknowledging its artfulness is to retain the contents and most of the structure of the tale, but then divert them into a realm where art *can* hide: for example, to turn the Märchen into a legend, a story told as true, or into a joke that mocks (even as it parades) the magic of the Märchen. As many as one-third of the most popular mountain Märchen plots and most characteristic performances do exactly this, translating Märchen into legend or joke form.

I here invoke a third tale, retold by a third writer, to underscore a third trait of the oral Märchen that has been seriously misrepresented in most published Märchen collections. The date is 1955, the teller Vance Randolph, who, like Richard Chase, was an outsider with literary ambitions who fell under the spell of the mountains (the Ozarks of northern Arkansas and southern Missouri). Randolph first visited this area in 1899 as a child of seven and returned in 1920 to spend the next sixty years there (Cochran 1985:13–14, 64, 67–68).

Chase's life and work more than suggest that hit-and-run collecting will ultimately favor the exhibitionist, leaving the less limelight-centered artists in the dark; furthermore, Chase's case illustrates how our emphasis on the most obvious tradition and most flamboyant performances has denied folklorists knowledge of and access to shyer narrative traditions. Vance Randolph seems to have agreed. In an interview toward the end of his life, he said, "[Richard M.] Dorson came down here once to Pine Bluff and he collected more tales in two weeks than I would get in a year. But I've always thought that he got the more superficial stuff, more off-the-top-of-the-head stuff. He could never have got some of the stuff I did, but, hell, I stayed fifty years" (Randolph 1978).

The notes to Randolph's tales back him up. Randolph didn't find Rose Spaulding, his finest and most prolific Märchen teller, until he'd been living in the Ozarks and collecting more than thirty years. The remaining two of his three major Märchen tellers were lifelong friends. Randolph's Märchen emerged from longstanding, intimate, even deeply private relationships.

While waiting out the more straightforward Märchen, Randolph had little trouble finding Märchen transformed into legends, tall tales, and jokes, and it was through these altered forms that he came to know, imitate, and master the mountain Märchen's most public voice. If telling a magical tale manifestly to inspire wonder is a source of embarrassment, Randolph's sources and Randolph himself could tell a Märchen sideways, letting art in through the back door, creating magic through undercutting.

An example of the anti-magic strain of Randolph's art appears in "The Toadfrog," his version of "The Frog Prince," which ends as a father discovers his daughter in bed with a handsome young man. The girl tells her father the happy news about how she has saved the poor boy from the fate of being a frog "and the old man didn't believe that story, any more than you do" (1955). This is essential Randolph, cynical to the core and very funny at the same time, but this ending represents, more broadly, something about the pragmatic vein of American oral artistry. Randolph, like Chase, aspired to artistry and, like Chase, he undoubtedly changed the tales of his sources to suit his own aesthetic. The great difference between the two men is that Randolph's aesthetic was largely based upon and generally shared with his sources, who became in many cases his lifelong friends, while Chase's tales, like Chase himself, were generally spurned by his sources (McNeil 1999; Lindahl 1994a; Perdue 1987).

Perhaps most American Märchen have, over time, been supplanted by or shifted into other forms after the manner of Randolph's artful parodies. But there remains a significant strain of mountain folk fiction that fits squarely in the category of Märchen, in which the best and most representative tellers of these tales create powerful effects by calling attention away from their art. Their dominant style is a deadpan that refuses to acknowledge the magic or the beauty of the Märchen, a style shared with the understated quips characteristic of rural American humor in many contexts.

It is precisely with such diction that Edgar Ashley of Grassy Creek, North Carolina, told the tale of "Billy Peg and His Bull" (Glassie 1964). After his beloved bull died, in Ashley's words, Billy Peg "cried for nine days and nine nights and then he was hungry." In this one sentence, the inflationary magic of the Märchen and the homely practicality of the mountain context meet in comic harmony.

Conclusion

The Appalachian and Ozark tellers who decided to stick with the Märchen have developed and sustained a powerful type of oral art whose most special effects are almost totally lost in the published and performed adaptations that are now taken to represent the form. As far as literary productions are concerned, the much more faithful renderings of Leonard Roberts are almost entirely unacknowledged. Vance Randolph captured in writing, insofar as anyone can, some of the most elusive and least translatable aspects of these tales, proving that literature does not have to misrepresent its oral sources. But Chase's unintentional parodies—in which Jack appears as a tall tale hero with swagger and without subtlety, and in which the most intimate aspects of context and motivation are lost—continue to be taken as representative of the field.

The past decade has been marked by an explosion of interest in oral storytelling, but here, as well, mountain Märchen have been represented principally by alien and extreme styles, in which overstatement and sweeping gestures, rather than the quiet indirection of carefully crafted words and unexplained images, have prevailed. The best thing that can be said about such skewed representations is that they have diverted the crowds from mountain firesides and bedsides, allowing a shy tradition to persist more or less undisturbed. As folklorists committed to the goal of helping to vocalize folk communities on their own terms—a goal as necessary to pursue as it is impossible to achieve[7]—we are finally, after sixty years, rediscovering the tales and styles that preceded the parodies of Richard Chase and that continue to survive him.

University of Houston
Texas

Acknowledgments

Research for this essay was supported by the Virginia Foundation for the Humanities (VFH), which provided me with a fellowship in 1997 to study Appalachian Märchen. Chuck and Nan Perdue of the University of Virginia and Garry Barrow of VFH helped me use university and foundation resources to advantage. A 1998 Parsons Grant from the American Folklife Center (AFC) at the Library of Congress allowed me to extend that research. For aiding my work at the AFC, I thank Thea Austen, Jennifer Cutting, Judith Gray, Stephanie Hall, Joe Hickerson, Ann Hoog, Alan Jabbour, and David Taylor. I thank Gordon McKinney and Harry Rice of Berea College for their assistance and for encouraging my work with the Leonard Roberts Collection. My greatest debt is to Glen Anderson, Jane Muncy Fugate, Mark Fugate, Robert Fugate, and Hope Muncy and other members of their family, for extending their hospitality and generously sharing with me their tales and their memories.

Notes

1. By my count, the fifteen major collections are those of James Taylor Adams (1993), Isabel Gordon Carter (1925), Richard Chase (1943, 1948, 1956), Emelyn E. Gardner (1937), Maud Long (1955), Charles L. Perdue Jr. (1987), Vance Randolph (1952, 1955, 1957, 1958), and Leonard Roberts (1955, 1969, 1974). Gardner's is the only collection that is not of Ozark or southern Appalachian origin. Here, I omit Marie Campbell's substantial collection from the Appalachians of Kentucky (1958) because experts, believing that the tales were based very closely on book tales rather than on oral performances, have expressed significant doubts concerning the collection's faithfulness as a record of a living Märchen community. As Herbert Halpert puts it, "One of the American folktale collections regarded with great doubt by many scholars is Marie Campbell's *Tales from the Cloud Walking Country,* because most of its tales are very close to the Grimms' Household Tales" (personal correspondence February 25, 1991). Halpert goes on to suggest that Campbell may not have simply rewritten the Grimms, as some have suggested, but rather tapped a print-derived oral tradition. Campbell's collections should be thoughtfully re-examined, but until such a reassessment is complete, I find it best to exclude it from this survey.

2. For a general description of "the systemic qualities of a folk narrative," see El-Shamy 1979 and 1999.

3. See, for example, Ellis's evaluation of the tales of Maud Long (1994), who supplied the best-known Jack tales in the Library of Congress collections and the only ones to have been released in recorded form to the general public (Long 1955). As Ellis's comments pertain directly to my comparison of the styles of Richard Chase and Sam Harmon, I here quote him at length:

> [T]he "new" tales [i.e., Maud Long's performances recorded in 1947 by Duncan Emrich] that the Library of Congress released were actually learned from or modeled after Chase's literary versions. Long's recording of "Jack and the Giants' New Ground" differs from Jane Gentry's [Maud's mother, from whom she learned her tales] "Jack the Giant Killer" in many ways, while it agrees closely with Chase's "Jack in the Giants' New Ground," even reproducing dialogue word for word. Likewise, her "Jack and the Varmints" clearly departs from the bawdy Gentry tradition, in which the hero wears a belt labeled "Stiff Dick killed seven at a lick." Chase obviously had encountered this version of the tale, as he admits that his hero's rhyme ("Strong man Jack killed seven at a whack") was his invention. The original, "given by all our informants," Chase says, "had to be altered for printing"(R. Chase, 1943, 192). Long also bowdlerizes the line. More tellingly, in "Fill, Bowl! Fill!" Chase admits to altering the king's final challenge from "Sing the bowl full" to "Sing the bowl full of *lies*"—a suggestion from Stith Thompson himself (R. Chase, 1943, 94, 193). "The point of singing the bowl full of lies," Chase admits, "seems to have been lost in the Ward-Harmon tradition." Long, following Chase, has Jack "sing the bowl full of lies." (Ellis 1994:101)

In his performance of "Stiff Dick," reprinted in this volume and analyzed in this essay, Sam Harmon uses the same "Stiff Dick" rhyme that Maud Long's mother had used when telling her the tale. In this and other respects (such as the ordering of episodes), Harmon's performance runs closer to Jane Gentry's version (Carter 1925:355–57) than does the recorded rendition of Jane's daughter Maud.

4. Compare, for example, the passage that follows Jack's capture of the boar in the versions rendered by Harmon and by Chase. Sam Harmon keeps the narrative focused on Jack by quickly explaining how the king killed the boar: "The king, he sent a fellow out there and shot it." In comparison to this eleven-word account, Chase expends 102 words, developing an entire scene in which the boar terrifies the king's men until Jack steps in to shoot it:

> When the king rode up there and saw it was that wild hog, he like to beat his horse to death gettin' back. Blowed his horn and fifty to sixty men came runnin' up. They took a lot of Winchester rifles and went on up to that old house; but they were so scared they wouldn't go close enough to get a shoot at it. So fin'ly Jack he went on down there, poked around with a rifle and shot two or three times. The old hog went to tearin' around and when it fell it had tore that house plumb down. (Chase 1943:61)

Chase's development conflicts with Harmon's portrayal of an accidental hero who can win only through his words. Indeed, in this passage, Chase's hero seems to me to be in conflict with Chase's own portrayal, as presented elsewhere in the same tale, in which Jack speaks courageously but does not act accordingly.

5. Gold, a source of vibrant imagery in the Grimms' collection (consider, for example, the golden ball that the princess loses in the first Grimm tale, "The Frog King" [AT 440]), is also the commonest source of positive imagery in the tales of the Muncy family (and, I believe, in mountain Märchen in general). Yet it is the wealth attending the gold, rather than its physical beauty, that dominates in most tellings (see, for example, Jane Muncy's version of "Merrywise," this volume). The only frequently told tale in the Muncy repertoire that mentions beauty at any length is "Rawhead and Bloodybones," a tale whose heroine is rewarded by having both her personal fragrance and her physical beauty enhanced. This is the only one of the sixteen Muncy family tales of which I am aware that dwells at any length on imagery of beauty.

6. The studies of Labrie and MacDonald focus on the importance of visual imagery for the narrator, and their conversations with master storytellers reveal many of the same techniques of mental imaging that Jane Muncy Fugate revealed to me in discussing her tales. Work still needs to be done on the importance of such imagery in creating lasting memories for passive listeners to oral performances. I have written an essay outlining some of the reasons for giving greater consideration to the role of imagery in engaging the audience and affecting their memories of the tale (Lindahl 1997b).

7. Postmodern theorists (Spivak 1989) and ethnographers (Tyler 1987) have repeatedly stated that it is impossible for one individual or group to represent another fully. I am in complete agreement with their findings, but I am not sympathetic with their solutions. Although Stephen Tyler and others speak of surrendering to a sort of mutually therapeutic "evocation" focused on the relationship between the collector and informant, it is my belief that as long as one labels oneself a folklorist, one must repeatedly attempt to become "outnumbered," to listen long enough to as many diverse community voices as possible, in order to come as close as possible to the ultimately unachievable goal of voicing the community on its own terms (for a lengthy discussion of these ideas, see Lindahl 1997a). Some of the greatest contributions to the study of oral storytelling (e.g., Dégh 1989; Glassie 1982) should give us sufficient reason to re-affirm that, even if total representation is impossible, the *goal* of representation is a worthy one.

References Cited

Adams, James Taylor
    1993   *Grandpap Told Me Tales: Memories of an Appalachian Childhood.* Big Stone Gap, Va.: Fletcher Dean.
Anderson, Glen Muncy, and Hope Muncy
    1997   Tape-recorded interview with Glenn Muncy Anderson and Hope Muncy. Danville, Ky. May 6. Recorded and transcribed by Carl Lindahl.
Campbell, Marie
    1958   *Tales from Cloud Walking Country.* Bloomington: Indiana University Press.
Carrière, Joseph M.
    1946   Review of *The Jack Tales,* by Richard Chase. *Journal of American Folklore* 59:74–77.

Carter, Isabel Gordon
  1925 "Mountain White Folklore: Tales from the Southern Blue Ridge." *Journal of American Folklore* 38:340–74.
Chase, Richard
  1943 *The Jack Tales.* Boston: Houghton Mifflin.
  1948 *Grandfather Tales.* Boston: Houghton Mifflin.
  1956 *American Folk Tales and Songs.* New York; reprint New York: Dover, 1971.
Cochran, Robert
  1985 *Vance Randolph: An Ozark Life.* Urbana and Chicago: University of Illinois Press.
Dégh, Linda
  1989 *Folktales and Society: Story-Telling in a Hungarian Peasant Community.* 2d ed. Bloomington: Indiana University Press.
Dunaway, Wilma A.
  1996 *The First American Frontier: Transition to Capitalism in Southern Appalachia, 1700–1860.* Chapel Hill: University of North Carolina Press.
Ellis, Bill
  1994 "The Gentry-Long Tradition and the Roots of Revivalism." In *Jack in Two Worlds: Contemporary North American Tales and Their Tellers,* ed. William Bernard McCarthy, 93–106. Chapel Hill: University of North Carolina Press.
El-Shamy, Hasan
  1979 *Brother and Sister: A Cognitive Behavioristic Analysis of a Middle Eastern Oikotype.* Folklore Monograph Series, No. 8. Bloomington: Folklore Publications Group.
  1999 *Tales Arab Women Tell.* Bloomington: Indiana University Press.
Fugate, Jane Muncy
  2000 Three days of interviews and folktale performances. Conducted, recorded, and transcribed by Carl Lindahl. Melbourne, Fla. June 2–4.
Gantz, Jeffrey
  1981 *Early Irish Myths and Sagas.* New York: Penguin.
Gardner, Emelyn E.
  1937 *Folklore from the Schoharie Hills, New York.* Ann Arbor: University of Michigan Press.
Glassie, Henry
  1964 "Three Southern Mountain Jack Tales." *Tennessee Folklore Society Bulletin* 30/3:78–94.
  1982 *Passing the Time in Ballymenone: Culture and History of an Ulster Community.* Philadelphia: University of Pennsylvania Press.
Grimm, Jakob, and Wilhelm Grimm
  1987 *The Complete Fairy Tales of the Brothers Grimm.* Trans. Jack Zipes. New York: Bantam.
Gutierrez, C. Paige
  1978 "The Jack Tale: A Definition of a Folk Tale Sub-Genre." *North Carolina Folklore Journal* 26/2:85–110.
Halpert, Herbert
  1939 Unpublished notes accompanying the 419 discs (AFS 2735—3153) recorded by Halpert during his collection expedition in the American

South, March 15–June 15, co-sponsored by the Library of Congress and the Folk Arts Committee of the Works Progress Administration. Washington, D.C.: American Folklife Center, Library of Congress.

Harmon, Samuel
1939   "Stiff Dick." Recorded by Herbert Halpert and transcribed by Carl Lindahl. Library of Congress, Archive of Folk Culture. Recordings. AFS #2924B–2925A.

Henry, Mellinger Edward
1938   *Folk-Songs from the Southern Highlands.* New York: J. J. Augustin.

Isbell, Robert
1996   *The Last Chivaree: The Hicks Family of Beech Mountain.* Chapel Hill: University of North Carolina Press.

Labrie, Vivian
1979   "Le Sabre de lumière et de vertu de sagesse: Anatomie d'une rémémoration." *Canadian Folklore Canadien* 1:37–70.
1981   "The Itinerary as a Possible Memorized Form of the Folktale." *ARV* 37: 89–102.

Lindahl, Carl
1994a   "Jacks: The Name, the Tales, the American Traditions." In *Jack in Two Worlds: Contemporary North American Tales and Their Tellers,* ed. William Bernard McCarthy, xiii–xxxiv. Chapel Hill: University of North Carolina Press.
1994b   "Jack, My Father, and Uncle Ray: Frank Proffitt, Jr." In *Jack in Two Worlds: Contemporary North American Tales and Their Tellers,* ed. William Bernard McCarthy, 27–33. Chapel Hill: University of North Carolina Press.
1997a   "The Power of Being Outnumbered." *Louisiana Folklore Miscellany* 12:43–75.
1997b   "The Oral Aesthetic and the Bicameral Mind." In *Gilgamesh: A Reader,* ed. John Maier. Wauconda, Ill.: Bolchazy-Carducci Publishers. Reprinted, with addendum, from *Oral Tradition* 6 (1991):120–26.
1999   "Jack Tales." In *Traditional Storytelling Today,* ed. Margaret Read MacDonald, 394–97. Chicago: Fitzroy Dearborn.

Long, Maud
1955   "Jack Tales." Two LP records, AAFS 47 and 48. Washington, D.C.: Archive of Folk Culture, Library of Congress.

Lüthi, Max
1986   *The Fairy Tale as Art Form and Portrait of Man.* Bloomington: Indiana University Press.

MacDonald, Donald Archie
1978   "A Visual Memory." *Scottish Studies* 22:1–26.

Massignon, Geneviève
1965   *Contes traditionnels des tailleurs de lin du Trégor.* Paris: A. et J. Picard.

McDermitt, Barbara
1983   "Storytelling and a Boy Named Jack." *North Carolina Folklore Journal* 31: 3–22.

McNeil, W. K.
1999   "Where Have All the Märchen Gone? Or, Don't They Tell Those Little Stories Any More?" In *Traditional Storytelling Today,* ed. Margaret Read MacDonald, 387–93. Chicago: Fitzroy Dearborn.

Nicolaisen, W. F. H.
  1978 "English Jack and American Jack." *Midwest Journal of Language and Folk-lore* 4: 27–36.
  1994 "The Teller and the Tale: Storytelling on Beech Mountain." In *Jack in Two Worlds: Contemporary North American Tales and Their Tellers,* ed. William Bernard McCarthy, 123–49. Chapel Hill: University of North Carolina Press.
Opie, Peter, and Iona Opie
  1974 *The Classic Fairy Tales.* New York: Oxford University Press.
Perdue, Charles L., Jr.
  1987 *Outwitting the Devil: Jack Tales from Wise County Virginia.* Santa Fe: Ancient City Press.
Randolph, Vance
  1952 *Who Blowed Up the Church House? and Other Ozark Folk Tales.* New York: Columbia University Press.
  1955 *The Devil's Pretty Daughter and Other Ozark Folk Tales.* New York: Columbia University Press.
  1957 *The Talking Turtle and Other Ozark Folk Tales.* New York: Columbia University Press.
  1958 *Sticks in the Knapsack and Other Ozark Folk Tales.* New York: University Press.
  1978 Interview, conducted by Richard S. Tallman. Original housed in Arkansas College Folklore Archive, Batesville.
Roberts, Leonard
  1949–80 Leonard Roberts Collection. Hutchins Library, Berea College. Berea, Ky.
  1955 *South from Hell-fer-Sartin: Kentucky Mountain Folktales.* Lexington: University Press of Kentucky.
  1969 *Old Greasybeard: Tales from the Cumberland Gap.* Philadelphia; reprint Pikeville, Ky.: Pikeville College Press, 1980.
  1974 *Sang Branch Settlers.* Austin; reprint Pikeville, Ky.: Pikeville College Press, 1980.
Spivak, Gyatri
  1989 "Can the Subaltern Speak?" In *Marxist Interpretations of Literature and Culture: Limits, Frontiers, Boundaries.* Urbana and Chicago: University of Illinois Press.
Tatar, Maria
  1987 *The Hard Facts of the Grimms' Fairy Tales.* Princeton: Princeton University Press.
Tyler, Stephen
  1987 *The Unspeakable: Discourse, Dialogue, and Rhetoric in the Postmodern World.* Madison: University of Wisconsin Press.
Utley, Francis Lee
  1975 "Oral Genres as a Bridge to Written Literature." In *Folklore Genres,* ed. Dan Ben-Amos, 3–15. Austin and London: University of Texas Press.
Updike, John
  1981 Review of Italo Calvino, *Fiabe Italiane. New Yorker,* Feb. 23: 120–26.
Woestendiek, Jo
  1990 Interview with Ray Hicks. *Winston Salem Journal,* July 22: A9, A12.

Two Transcriptions of "Jack and the Bull," by Polly Johnson

The following versions of "Jack and the Bull"(AT 511A: The Little Red Ox) were collected simultaneously (on October 13, 1941) by James Taylor Adams and Richard Chase from Mrs. Polly Johnson of Wise, Virginia. Adams and Chase worked together as part of the Virginia Writers' Project, a program sponsored and funded by the Work Projects Administration during 1941 and 1942 (see Perdue 1987:96–116). Mrs. Johnson said that she had learned the tale from her mother. In his notes to this tale, Adams commented, "This is the first time I have heard this tale outside the Adams family."

The texts below represent the original transcriptions (first published in Perdue 1987:14–21), and one can readily see that Adams's transcription is almost twice as long as Chase's version. It would appear that Chase wrote down the basic tale and only later, for publication, elaborated upon it and brought in parts of other versions of the same tale. "Jack and the Bull" as published in *The Jack Tales* (Chase 1943) was collated from versions told by Mrs. Johnson, Mr. and Mrs. James Taylor Adams, Finley Adams, and Mrs. Nancy Shores.

Polly Johnson of Wise, Virginia. Mrs. Johnson narrated "Jack and the Bull" as transcribed here by James Taylor Adams and Richard Chase. *Courtesy Mrs. Johnson's granddaughter, Estelle Varner.*

Charles L. Perdue Jr.
University of Virginia

99

"Jack and The Bull"
as told by Polly Johnson, October 13, 1941, and transcribed by
James Taylor Adams

One time there was a pore boy. His name was Jack an' he worked fer a rich family. The old man liked Jack, but the old woman jis hated him. She would send Jack to feed the cattle ever time jis about when she got sump'n to eat ready. Jack was jis goin' to skin an' bones. Nearly starved to death.

One day a strange bull come along an' jumped in the field. An' that evenin' when Jack went to feed the cattle he was cryin'. The bull said, "What's the matter, Jack? What are ye cryin' about?" Jack told him the old woman was tryin' to starve him to death an' sent him to feed ever' time when she got sump'n to eat ready.

The bull said, "Don't worry Jack. You jis beat on my right horn an' you'll find cheese an' bread an' beat on my left horn an' you'll find milk an' butter." So Jack beat on his right horn an' there was all the bread an' cheese he wanted to eat an' he beat on the left horn an' thar was all the milk an' butter he could eat. So he went back to the house feelin' good. An' he begin to pick right up fer he eat that way ever' day.

Wudn't long tell the old woman noticed he was gainin' flash an' she wondered what was the reason. So she had two boys. One was a two-eyed boy an' the other was a three-eyed boy. She sent the two-eyed boy to watch an' see where Jack was gittin' his eatin's. Now Jack he was a fiddler. An' when he seed the two-eyed boy thar watchin' him he took his fiddle an' set down upon the bank an' started playin'. He played an' he played tell one eye was played to sleep an' he played an' he played till the other eye was played to sleep an' then he beat on the bull's horns an' got his supper.

So the two-eyed boy waked up after while an' went back an' told his mother he didn't see a thing. So she sent the three-eyed boy to watch. An' Jack he took his fiddle an' set down on the bank an' started playin'. He played an' he played an' played the eye to sleep. An' he played an' he played an' played another eye to sleep. An' he played an' he played an' he played but he couldn't never git the third eye played to sleep. He was gittin' mighty hungry an' he went over an' beat on the bull's horns an' eat his supper an' the three eyed boy seed him out of the one eye he hadn't played to sleep an' he went back an' told his mammy.

So the next day she told her old man that she was longin' fer that strange bull's liver an' lights [the lungs] an' he'd have to kill him an' git his liver an' lights fer her. He didn't want to do it, but she kept right on an' on. Finally he told Jack he'd have to kill the strange bull an' git his liver an' lights fer his wife. Jack went to the field that evenin' a cryin'. The bull said, "What's wrong now, Jack?" He told him that the old woman had found out where he was gittin' his eatin's an' had made up her mind to have his liver an' lights.

James Taylor Adams (1892–1954), also from Wise County, Virginia, collected tales in 1941 and 1942 while employed by the WPA's Virginia Writers' Project. This photo appeared in *Virginia Cavalcade* 21/4, Spring 1972.

The bull told Jack not to worry, that he'd jump on one of the cows an' kill her and they'd git her liver an' lights an' let Jack take 'em to the old woman an' she'd not know the difference. So he did, an' Jack took the liver an' lights an' give 'em to the old woman an' then he went back an' the bull told him to climb up on his back an' he'd carry him to safety. An' Jack got up on his back an' they traveled an' traveled on an' traveled on.

One mornin' they got up an' the bull looked bothered. Jack axed him what was the matter, an' he told Jack he'd had a bad dream. Said he had dreamed they was goin' along an' met up with a two-headed bull an' him an' the two-headed bull had fit an' fit but that he had finally whuped the two-headed bull.

So they went on an' on an' shore enough that day they met up with a two-headed bull an' Jack got off his bull's back an' crawled up on the bank an' they went to fightin'. They fit an' they fit. Lot o' times Jack thought the ol' two-headed bull was goin' to kill his bull, but finally his bull whuped him. An' got on his bull an' they went on.

The next mornin' the bull looked more bothered than ever. Jack wanted to know what was the matter. An' he told Jack he'd dreamed they met a three-headed bull an' they had a fight an' he killed him. He tol' Jack 'f they did meet a three-headed bull an' he got killed fer him to skin a strip from the tip of his tail to his head an' take off his horns an' take it with him, an' any time he was in trouble to jis say:

"Tie, strap, tie.
Beat, horns, beat!"

an' he would git anything he wanted.

So they went on an' shore enough they met up with a big three-headed bull an' Jack got off of his bull's back an' clomb on the bank an' they started fightin'. They fit an' they fit an' at last the three-headed bull killed his bull an' went on up the road bellowin'. Jack got down an' took out his pocketknife an' skun a strip from the end's his bull's tail to the tip of his nose an' took off his horns an' went on. When he got hungry all he had to do was beat on the horns an' git his eatin's.

He went on an' on an' finally one day he stopped at a house where an' old woman lived an' she wanted to hire him to herd sheep fer her. He took the job an' all the neighbors told him he couldn't git along with her that she was contrary an' mean. But he worked on till one day she come out where he was an' said, "Jack, which do you chose, hard gripes or sharp shins." He told her he believed he'd rather have hard gripes. So she jumped on him an' started chokin' him. He hollered out "Tie, strap, tie, Beat, horns, beat!" An' the strap tied her down an' the horns set in to beatin' her. She couldn't stan' that so she tol' Jack to take 'em off an' she buy him a new suit of clothes. So Jack took 'em off. An' hit went on a few days an' the old woman didn't bother him any more. Then she come out where he was at ag'in an' said, "Jack, which do you chose, hard gripes or sharp shins?" Jack said, "Hard gripes." An' she jumped on him ag'in an' begin choking him. He hollered, "Tie, strap, tie. Beat, horns, beat!" An' the strap tied her down an' the horns set in beatin' her an' was about to beat her to death an' she told Jack 'f he'd take 'em off she'd give him a pocketbook full of gold. So Jack told 'em to let her alone an' they did.

So hit went on fer a week or two an' the ol' woman didn't pester Jack any more. But one day she come to where he was workin' an' said, "Jack, which do you chose, hard gripes or sharp shins?" He told her hard gripes, an' she jumped on him an' begin chokin' him. He hollered, "Tie, strap, tie. Beat, horns, beat!" an' the strap tied her down an' the horns set in beatin' her an' this time they had her nearly beat to death when she started hollerin' fer Jack to take 'em off an' she'd give him a fine hoss, bridle an' saddle. An' he did.

So Jack put on his new suit, put his pocketbook full of gold in his pocket an' got on his hoss an' started out. He was goin' along one day when he seed a lot of people out in a big bottom aroun' a ball set on top of a pole. They had a slick board laid up ag'inst the pole an' a lot of young men was tryin' to ride their hosses up the plank. Jack stopped an' went over an' axed 'em what they was doin'. They told him the King had agreed to give any man his daughter that would ride his hoss to the top of the pole and bring back the ball.

Jack axed 'em 'f he could try an' they said yes, hit was free fer all. So Jack he got back on his hoss an' takin' the strap an' horns of his bull in his hands he put the spurs to his hoss an' hollered,

> "Tie, strap, tie.
> Beat, horns, beat."

An' the strap stretched out an' tied aroun' the top of the pole an' the horns hooked his hoss an' he went right on up the plank to the top of the pole an' Jack got the ball an' come down, an' the King's daughter welcomed him at the bottom, an' they married an' was happy.

"Jack and the Bull"
as told by Polly Johnson, October 13, 1941,
and transcribed by Richard Chase

There was a boy by the name of Jack. Was a poor boy. He got work herdin' cattle for some folks. They wouldn't feed him. He was about to starve. A strange bull come and jumped into the lot with the cows. Said to Jack, "Jack, I see you're starvin'. You watch till that boy turns his back. Then you beat on my right horn and you'll get bread and cheese, and beat on my left horn and you'll get milk and butter." So Jack watched and eat from the bull's horns, and he was gettin' fat and full. The old woman had two boys. She saw Jack gettin' fat so she sent her two-eyed boy to watch. Jack got his fiddle and played one eye to sleep. Then he played the other eye to sleep. And eat from the bull's horns. The old woman sent her boy with three eyes. Jack played two eyes to sleep, but he couldn't play that last eye to sleep. He got so hongry he went on and knocked on the bull's horns. The boy seed Jack knock on the horns and get bread and cheese and milk and butter. So he told the old woman, and she told her man she wanted that bull's liver and lights. The old man says, "Jack, we'll have to kill that bull." Jack told the bull, and he says, "Now Jack, I'll jump on one of those cows and knock out her liver and lights." So he hooked her and killed her. Jack took the cow's liver and lights to the old man, says, "Here's that old devil bull's liver and lights." The bull told Jack, "Set on my back and we'll leave." So he did, and they travelled on, and travelled on, and travelled on. They went to sleep and the bull dreamed of meetin' another bull. Says, "I'll whip him." They met the bull and Jack's bull whuped him. That night they went to sleep again, and the bull says, "Jack, I dreamed a bad dream. Met a bull with two heads. Finally I whuped him." They went on and heard the bull. Jack hid and watched 'em fight. Jack's bull whuped the other one. They travelled on that day. And next morning Jack's bull says, "Jack, I dreamed a worser dream last night. Met a bull with three heads, and he whuped me this time. We'll meet him today. When you hear that bull you hide. And when he kills me you wait till he goes away, then you skin a strop from the end of my tail plumb up my back and git my horns so you'll git your vittles just the same." So they met that bull with three heads. And they fit and fit, and he killed Jack's bull. So Jack skun a strop from the end of his tail to his horns and got the horns. Jack went on and he was gettin' all raggedy. He come to where there was an old woman. She was a witch. He got him a job. She said, "I'll hire you to herd sheep." The folks told Jack, "Jack, you'll never see no peace with that old woman. Can't nobody get along with her." Jack says, "I'll stand her off." She come to him, says, "Do you want hard gripes or sharp shins?" He told her he'd take hard gripes. So she went to fight him, and he says, "Tie strop, tie! Beat horns, beat!" So the strop tied the old woman and the horns went to beatin' her, and she hollered. "Let me up and I'll buy you a fine suit of clothes." So Jack let her up. Next day she came right back. Asked him did he want hard gripes or sharp shins. Jack downed her, tied her down and like to beat her to death. "Let me up, Jack, I'll give you a pocketbook full of gold and silver." Jack said all right. Next morning she come again, says, "Hard gripes or sharp shins?" Jack tuk hard gripes and the strop tied her and the horns beat her till she hollered and begged for Jack to let her up and she'd give him a (sure-footed -?-) horse and a bridle and saddle. So Jack tuk his suit of fine clothes and his pocket book and his horse and saddle and bridle, and went on off to seek his fortune. He come to where there was a ball put high up there. And they'd grease a plank and whoever could make a horse go up that plank would get so much money and get the King's daughter. Jack made his horse go up to the plank. And they said, "He'll not get that." Jack rode right up and got the ball. Then Jack put on his old raggedy clothes and went to soppin' in the pots. They commenced to beatin' him, says, "Get out of here." Then that ball fell out of his pocket and the King's girl saw it, says, "I know who's got the ball." She told 'em it was Jack. So Jack got on his fine suit of clothes and come in like a fine feller again. And Jack got to marry her.

Storybook Style: "Jack and the Green Man"

Like the more elaborate Märchen of the Muncy family (see "Merry-wise," this volume), the following tale is inflected with literary diction. "Jack and the Green Man" borrows extensively from the vocabulary of storybooks and nursery rhymes, as in the mention of "the butcher, the baker, and the candlestick maker" in the opening sentence and in references to "courtiers," "waistcoats," "palaces," and other storybook characters, props, and scenery conspicuously absent from the well-known tales of the Hicks-Harmon family. Although the major early collectors of Appalachian Märchen tended to ignore such genteel performances, this tale presents evidence—together with many of the un-published tales in the Roberts collection and some of the Muncy family's favorite tales— for a significant Appalachian tradition of Märchen influenced by literary styles.

"Jack and the Green Man" offers an interesting comparison to several versions of the same tale published in *Outwitting the Devil: Jack Tales from Wise County Virginia* (see "Willie and the Devil" and "Jack and Old King Morock," in Perdue 1987:28–50). The tale also suggests a hitherto undiscovered point of continuity between Appalachian and Newfoundland Märchen traditions. The present text is an example of one of the most popular tale types in Appalachia: AT 313, "The Girl as Helper in the Hero's Flight." Yet this is, to our knowledge, the only American text in which the villain is a green man. Giant men are popular antagonists in Irish and Scottish versions of this tale, and Halpert and Widdowson have published several variants of AT 313 in which a green man appears (see tales 7–13 and the extensive accompanying notes in Halpert and Widdowson, *Folktales of Newfoundland* [1996]).

The version published here was included in a paper for a folklore course by University of Virginia student Katherine Griffin. She stated in her paper that this tale, along with two others, had "been handed down for at least five known generations" of her family in Virginia. She introduced the story with the following comments:

In 1945 Louise Fontaine Mann, then around sixty years old, wrote down three stories, including Jack and the Green Man. I have no way of knowing how much the stories had changed when she set them down in writing, nor of their origin. I remember hearing about Jack's talking bean, and whenever I would make plans to run away, I would always wish that I had a talking bean that would say that

106

I was still upstairs when actually I had been gone all afternoon. (Griffin, 1974-47, "Collection of Family Folklore," in the Kevin Barry Perdue Archive of Traditional Culture, University of Virginia)

Carl Lindahl   Charles L. Perdue Jr.
University of Houston   University of Virginia

"Jack and the Green Man"
as written down by Louise Fontaine Mann, 1945

Once upon a time a king lived with his courtiers on one side of a river; the butchers, bakers, and the candlestick makers lived on the other side and brought necessities over a bridge to the palace each day. One morning, to the great discomfort of all, the bridge was found broken down; so the king set the army to rebuild it. The soldiers could not quite finish the bridge, so they set a guard at each end of it and went home to bed. Next morning the soldiers were gone and the bridge was destroyed as before. They set to work, but they could not quite finish, and this time they asked for volunteers to guard the bridge. The king's son Jack stepped forward and said he would do it. The king was displeased with the idea, but could not refuse; so Jack took up his position as sentinel on the bridge.

Nothing happened till just at midnight a huge bull came trotting up. He stamped and he ramped on the bridge until it shook to its foundation. When Jack saw what the bull was doing he rushed onto the bridge, and, pulling a pearl-handled pistol from its holster, shot the bull right between the eyes. A small drop of blood appeared and the bull took a white handkerchief out of his waistcoat pocket, wiped away the blood, and trotted down the road.

He was hardly out of sight when a little man appeared, dressed all in green, and said, "What do you mean by shooting at my bull?" "And what do you mean by letting your bull destroy my father's bridge?" said Jack. The Green Man said, "Let's settle that by fighting, and whoever wins will be the other's master." So they took off their coats, and the Green Man's little dog took charge of his clothes. They fought and they fought, and Jack couldn't beat the Green Man and the Green Man couldn't beat Jack. They sat down to catch their breath and decided to play cards to see who would be the master. They played and they played, but Jack couldn't beat the Green Man and the Green Man couldn't beat Jack, until the Green Man directed his little dog to hold a mirror in his mouth behind Jack so he could see Jack's cards and beat him. "So I've beat you," said the Green Man, "and I will be your master." Jack agreed. "Yes," he said, "You've beat me." So it was arranged that Jack should stay at home for a year and a day, after which he was to go to the Green Man's country and serve him. The Green Man did not really want Jack, but thought he would get rid of him by putting him off so long.

However, when the time came, Jack set out to keep his word and to look for the Green Man's country. He traveled all day till he found a man working on the road and asked him the way. The man said, "Why do you want to go there? He is a bad man—a conjuror." Jack said he knew that, but that he had promised. "Well," said the man, "then you will have to go, but if you are going there you will need a friend. The Green Man and his wife have a daughter named Susan. Susan is not their real daughter, but a child they stole as an infant. You will do very well to make Susan your friend. Beyond those trees over there is a lake and right now Susan is bathing in it. Her clothes are on the bank. Just you hide and keep them till she promises to be your friend."

Jack followed his instructions, and Susan retired behind a tree, dressed, and they started together for the Green Man's house. Then Jack and Susan separated and Jack reported to the Green Man, "Here I am. What are you going to do with me?"

The Green Man set Jack to cleaning his stable, which hadn't been cleaned for forty years, telling him to look for his grandmother's ring, lost there forty years before. Jack started out with the Green Man's spade, but for every shovel full that he threw out at the door a wagon load came in at the window. Jack saw something was wrong and went straight to Susan. "Ah," said she, "You were right to come to me—it's because you have the Green Man's spade." And she gave him a silver spade, which worked well; for when he threw out a spade full at the door a wagon load went out of the window, and there was the ring sticking in a crack.

The Green Man and his wife talked it over that night, and she told him to have Jack saddle the Five Mile Colt. So next day the Green

Man gave Jack a bridle and told him to do it. Jack found that as soon as he approached the colt it jumped five miles; so again he went for help to Susan, who gave him a silver bridle, and with its help he soon had the colt in the Green Man's stable.

That night the Green Man and his wife discussed the matter, and he said to her, "That boy isn't as stupid as I thought him. He does everything I tell him." The Green Man's wife said, "I believe Susan helps him." This enraged the Green Man so that he vowed to kill them both.

Susan overheard this plot and made her plans, and she told Jack to saddle the Five Mile Colt and tie him in the bushes. She baked a cake, put into it a Talking Bean, and set it in the oven in her room upstairs to bake. Then she collected all the conjuring books, and she and Jack rode off with them on the Five Mile Colt.

Meanwhile the Green Man was sharpening his knife, while waiting for Susan and Jack to go to sleep. Presently he called upstairs, "Susan, are you asleep?" The cake had begun to bake and the Talking Bean was very hot; so it said in a loud voice, "No Sir!" So the Green Man waited awhile, still sharpening his knife, and then he called again, "Susan: are you asleep?" The cake was done now, and the fire low, so the Talking Bean answered this time in a small voice, "No Sir." "Ah," said the Green Man—satisfaction in his voice—"She'll soon be asleep now." So he waited awhile longer, still sharpening his knife, and then he called upstairs, "Susan!! Are you asleep?" Now the cake was done and the fire was out, and the Talking Bean was only slightly warm; so it only whispered, "No Sir," and the Green Man couldn't hear it. So the Green Man crept upstairs to make an end of Susan, and there was no Susan and no Jack. He called his wife, who told him to saddle the Five Mile Colt while she consulted the conjuring books to see where the two had gone, saying, "We'll soon have them back." But in five minutes they were back in the kitchen with the news that the Five Mile Colt was gone, and the conjuring books too, all but one leaf that had been blown into a gutter.

Meanwhile Jack and Susan had gotten a long way off, when Susan said, "Jack! Look behind you—what do you see?" Jack said, "I see a great forest of trees coming up behind us." "Oh," said Susan, who had studied the conjuring books, "that is the Green Man and his wife. Look in the colt's right ear." He found there a rusty nail, and, by Susan's direction, threw it behind him, when it turned into an army of woodcutters who promptly chopped down the forest, and Jack and Susan rode on. Presently Susan again grew anxious and again said, "Jack! Look behind you—what do you see?" Jack looked back and said, "I see a great river rushing toward us." Susan said, "Quick—look in the colt's left ear." Jack saw there a small phial of water which, again by Susan's direction, he uncorked and threw behind them. It turned into a lake, and swallowed up the river, and almost immediately they reached the end of the Green Man's country, and were safe.

When they stopped at an inn for supper, Susan said she was not sure of her welcome at the palace, and told Jack to go home without her and prepare the way, but he must not let anyone kiss him there, or he would forget all about her. Jack disguised himself as an old man, but when he got home the dear old house dog knew him anyway and jumped up and kissed him, so that he did forget all about Susan.

After awhile a wedding was arranged for Jack with a neighboring princess, and Susan, waiting and grieving, heard about it. So she made a plan. On the wedding day a message was brought to Jack that there was an old woman in the courtyard with a covered basket, who urgently wished to show him her talking chickens. Jack sent word that it was impossible—he was just ready to be married. Word came back that he would regret it all his life if he did not see her; so, as Jack had a kind heart, he excused himself from his bride and went down to the courtyard. There was the old woman with a shawl pulled over her head so he could not see her face. She said no word to Jack, but threw some corn on the ground, took the top off the basket, and out hopped a rooster and a hen. The rooster gobbled up all the corn without leaving any for the hen, and Jack heard a voice saying, very low, "Ah, Jack, how *could* you forget poor Susan?" And with the name Susan Jack jumped forward and pulled the shawl from her face, and there was Susan, whereupon everything came back to him.

He took her by the hand and led her to his father, telling him all about it, and they all agreed that of course he couldn't marry anyone but Susan. The princess didn't much care; so they all lived happily ever after, and never forgot to help the poor.

Charles L. Perdue Jr.

Is Old Jack Really Richard Chase?

In 1958 I was a student at the University of California, Berkeley, majoring in geology. My wife Nan and I had two young children, one three years old and the other nine months. We regularly spent Saturday evenings with friends at the Blind Lemon coffee house, singing folksongs and drinking cheap wine and beer to relieve the stressful circumstances of schoolwork, a young family, and living on the GI Bill, supplemented by multiple part-time jobs. On one such evening in the spring of 1958, we walked into the Blind Lemon and found a man sitting in the corner and telling a long, drawn-out tale about a character named Jack. We had come to sing, but we waited politely until the tale had ended and then began to get out our instruments—only to hear another tale begin. This was, we thought, our turf—so we began singing loudly. The man cut his tale short and left in a huff. This was our introduction (we learned later) to Richard Chase and Jack tales.

My interest in folklore, rooted in childhood and personal experience, developed and grew into a professional interest after I entered the Ph.D. program in folklore at the University of Pennsylvania in the fall of 1967. An interest that Nan and I both had in the Great Depression of the 1930s (having experienced it first hand) also developed and led, eventually, to the discovery of twenty-eight Jack tales collected by workers on the WPA's Virginia Writers' Project. Preparation of those tales for publication as *Outwitting the Devil: Jack Tales from Wise County, Virginia* led us back to Richard Chase.

As Chase describes in *The Jack Tales* (1943), he became aware of the oral Jack Tale tradition in the spring of 1935 when he was hired to teach folksongs at a teachers' conference sponsored by the Office of Emergency Relief in Raleigh, North Carolina. His account of learning about the tradition from Marshall Ward has varied as much as the

Jack tales themselves. In a 1939 article on the origins of the Jack tales, Chase wrote that Ward approached him after his talk at the conference and said, "My family knows some old stories that have been handed down from generation to generation, like you were saying about the old songs. I don't know whether you'd be interested in any such old tales or not." Chase assured him that he was interested and asked what these old stories were like. "Well," he said, "they're mostly about a boy named Jack" (Chase 1939b).

Even in relating the history of this first encounter with Ward in subsequent publications, Chase's tendency to emendation can be seen. In 1943, Chase reports the story much as he did in the 1939 article, with the significant exception of Ward's answer to the question "What sort of stories are they?" This time, Ward replies, "They're mostly about a boy named Jack, and his two brothers, Will and Tom" (Chase 1943). Finally, in 1962, during a talk at Appalachian State University, Chase situated Marshall Ward as an Appalachian character himself by placing his words in a perceived-to-be-mountain dialect:

> This boy [Ward was twenty-six years old at the time and college educated; Chase was twenty-eight] came up to me and said, "We'ens knows some old tales handed down from generation to generation, like the saying about the songs—My folks up near Boone." And I said, "What kind of tales?" "Ah, they're mostly about a boy named Jack." I said, "Jack and the beanstalk." He said, "Yea, well, that's the way it's in them school books. We'ens don't tell it that way." And I knew at once what I hit. I knew that was my destiny and I knew I had to do so (Chase 1962).

By September 1939 Chase had visited the Ward family twice and collected about thirty tales, including sixteen Jack tales. In an article on Marshall Ward, Cheryl Oxford notes that Ward's "greatest legacy" may have been "his contribution to Richard Chase's 1943 publication of *The Jack Tales.*" However, the accounts of Ward's influence differ as well. Ward says he met Chase at Appalachian State Teachers College in Boone, North Carolina—not Raleigh as Chase has it; Ward also states that he told Chase sixteen tales and that they, along with two tales "from other places . . . made up his Jack Tale book"(1994:56–69). However, Chase gives Ward credit for contributing to only *one* tale in *The Jack Tales.*

Much of the rest of Chase's life would be focused around the collection, publication, and performance of Jack tales. During the years

1935–1939, Chase had assumed that Jack tales were only to be found in North Carolina and he tried several times, without success, to obtain some financial assistance through the Recreation Division of the Work Projects Administration and other WPA programs for his tale-collecting work. In October 1940 Chase learned from R. M. Ward of Beech Creek, North Carolina, that Ward had been receiving folksongs, ballads, and tales in the mail from James Taylor Adams of Wise County, Virginia.[1]

In the year following, Chase put together a proposal to edit a book on Wise County folklore, got the Virginia Writers' Project to provide some travel funds, and began to type up outlines for the proposed Wise County book. His first letter to James Taylor Adams about the proposed book is dated September 19, 1941, and he made his first trip to Wise County on October 11. He followed that with another eight or so trips of two to four days each and ultimately spent about twenty-five days in the county between October 1941 and April 1942.[2]

During the same period in which Chase was gathering information for the Wise County book, he was also traveling and performing Punch and Judy shows and telling stories—including Jack tales—in several states. In addition, he did some work for the WPA's Recreation Division, refurbished a house in Albemarle County, Virginia, and, most importantly, completed work on *The Jack Tales*. Houghton Mifflin accepted the manuscript for that book in early May 1942.[3]

The Wise County book was never published, but much of what had been collected for that project saw print in *The Jack Tales* (1943), *Grandfather Tales* (1948), and *American Folk Tales and Songs* (1956). For the Wise County book Chase had created the fictive character of "Tom Hunt," clearly a pseudonym for himself—at least initially. In manuscript material for the projected Wise County book, dated November 26, 1941, Chase writes the following in a section he marks as "for opening materials":

> One reason Jeems [James Taylor Adams] and I got a better chance to go hunting for old tales and such was a fellow named Tom Hunt that came into Wise County every month for a while back there. Tom was a sort of writer like Jeems and had known Jeems a long while. He enjoyed the tales and old songs himself and he had a car, so whenever he came the rest of us could go out with him to visit certain places in the county we'd not be able to reach except by walkin' twenty or thirty miles.

> Tom Hunt was a sort of showman. He gave shows in schools with
> some little dolls he could put on his hands and work 'em like they were
> alive. There was Mister Punch and his wife Judy, and the devil was in it,
> too.[4]

Chase was not consistent in his presentation of the fictional Tom
Hunt. In *Grandfather Tales,* Tom Hunt became a local Wise Countian
who was visited by "James Turner" (James Taylor Adams) and "Dick
Chase"; Wise County became "Crockett County":

> It was on one of my first trips to Crockett County that James Turner took
> me out to see Tom Hunt. Mr. Hunt lives alone in an old hewn-log house
> about a mile out of the county seat. . . . [Turner says:] "Meet Dick Chase.
> He's in here huntin' up old songs and old tales." (Chase 1948:1–2)

The distinction between fiction and scholarship is further blurred
when, in annotating tales, Chase attributes a version of a tale to Tom
Hunt (Chase 1956:86).

By October 1941, when Chase made his first trip to Wise County,
ostensibly to collect material for the Wise County folklore book, the
Virginia Writers' Project was already beginning to close down its programs in preparation for the office's eventual closure in June 1942
(Martin-Perdue and Perdue 1996:360–80). It seems very likely that
Chase took advantage of an opportunity to gather more tales and
other material for his own publications, with a view to his having no
further obligation to produce the Wise County book after the VWP
closed its doors.

Chase, by his own statements, was unaware of the Jack tales prior
to his meeting with Marshall Ward in 1935, so he could not have had
any preconceived ideas about the character of Jack as an American
boy/hero. However, before *The Jack Tales* reached its final form in
1942, he *had* developed such a notion and he was shaping the tales—
consciously and perhaps unconsciously—to fit it. We know that Chase
did come to the Jack tales with the belief, shaped by his previous asso-
ciations with Cecil Sharp's English Folk Dance Society, that any traditional culture possessed by "Anglo-Saxon" people was the "racial inheritance" of all Anglo-Saxons—i.e., northern Europeans (Karpeles
1932:xxxvi).[5] And he became a missionary in the work of returning
that racial inheritance to white Americans—distilled, of course,
through his own psyche and experiences.

A young Richard Chase (1904–1988). The undated
photograph appeared in a brochure Chase sent (along
with a letter) to Spencer Adams, son of James Taylor
Adams, sometime after 1948. Both can be found in
The James Taylor Adams Papers, Box 47-C (II),
"Letters from Richard Chase," John Cook Wyllie
Library, Clinch Valley College, Wise, Virginia.

If one reads the notes to the Jack tales that Chase published between 1937 and 1956 and follows the republication of some of them
over time, it becomes clear that changes have been made. Chase's
practice in editing the tales is stated in the Preface to *The Jack Tales:*
"We have taken the best of many tellings and correlated the best of
all material collected into one complete version" (1943:xi). Whether
or not the changes he made are a product of his own mind, result
from different tellings by the same narrator or by others, or have

been added from published collections, it remains Chase's aesthetic that shapes the tales. Determining the nature of the changes that he made in the tales is further complicated by the fire that, according to Chase, destroyed his house in Beech Creek, North Carolina, and also destroyed any original copies he may have had of Jack tales he personally collected—at least twenty-four tales in North Carolina and thirteen in Wise County, Virginia.[6]

Comparative analysis of Jack tale collections can perhaps shed some light on the nature of Chase's editorial hand. My casual reading of Jack tales told by African Americans in the United States suggests that there might be significant differences between them and those told by white narrators, including those published by Richard Chase.[7] I constructed a list of aspects of the tales to see if it might be possible to perceive such differences and to describe them in a meaningful way. This work came to naught largely due to the paucity of published African American Jack tales from the continental United States. It occurred to me, however, that a similar trait analysis of Jack tales edited by Chase might reveal his contribution to the tales he published.

Chase may have developed his character of Jack over a period of time, and I initially thought it would be instructive to compare his earliest published tales in *Southern Folklore Quarterly* with versions of the same tales published a bit later in *The Jack Tales*. Chase does not give the dates when he collected the various tales but he does state in a 1939 article that he had made two collecting trips to the Beech Creek area and had collected twenty-four traditional tales. Sixteen of the tales were Jack tales and one can accurately assume that the tales published in *Southern Folklore Quarterly* were collected between the spring of 1935, when Chase met Marshall Ward, and the summer of 1939, when he was writing the article. Tales published in *The Jack Tales* were collected between the spring of 1935 and August 1, 1942, when Chase sent the final manuscript to Houghton-Mifflin Company. All of the tales published in *Southern Folklore Quarterly* were collected by Chase; some of the tales in *The Jack Tales* were collected by Chase, but in his collating of versions, he included material collected by James Taylor Adams, James M. Hylton, and possibly others, as well as material from tales previously published by an unknown number of collectors and editors. Table 1 indicates significant trait changes between the two sets of Chase's tales.

Table 1: Comparison of Jack Tales Published by Richard Chase in
Southern Folklore Quarterly (1937–1941) and *The Jack Tales* (1943)

Jack Tale Title	Southern Folklore Quarterly	The Jack Tales Completed July 1942; published Summer 1943
"Jack and the Giants" (Published in *SFQ* 1/1, March 1937)	Source: "written down from long-hand notes taken from the telling of it by R. M. (Monroe) Ward and his brother, Miles A. Ward, of Beech Creek, North Carolina." Traits: no family; does not go back to his home community	Source: R. M. Ward, Martha Ward Presnell, Roby Hicks, and Ben Hicks Traits: has a mother, father, and two brothers; goes back to his home community and is reunited with his family
"The Lion and the Unicorn" (Published in *SFQ* 1/4, December 1937)	Source: R. M. Ward, Miles A. Ward, and Ben Hicks, Beech Creek, North Carolina Traits: has a mother; is not lazy	Source: R. M. Ward, Miles A. Ward, Ben Hicks, and George Trivett Traits: no mother mentioned; is lazy
"Jack's Hunting Trip" (Published in *SFQ* 2/3, September 1938)	Source: R. M. Ward and Miles A. Ward Traits: has father, mother, and two brothers	Source: R. M. Ward, Miles A. Ward, and Roby Hicks Traits: has father only; tall tale added from VWP files, it was not a Jack tale but added to one
"Jack and the Bean Tree" (Published in *SFQ* 2/4, December 1938)	Source: R. M. Ward Traits: family is poor	Source: R. M. Ward, Ben Hicks, and Mrs. Martha Lethcoe of Damascus, Virginia Traits: family is not poor
"Lucky Jack" or "Fill, Bowl! Fill!" (Published in *SFQ* 3/1, March 1939)	Source: R. M. Ward Traits: Jack cuts off King's head and marries his daughter	Source: R. M. Ward Traits: Jack does not cut off King's head and does not marry his daughter; "of lies" is added to "sing this bowl full" (Motif H1045)
"Jack and the Fire Dragaman" (Published in *SFQ* 5/3, September 1941)	Source: R. M. Ward Traits: essentially unchanged	Source: R. M. Ward Traits: essentially unchanged

In summary, for the later version of "Jack and the Giants," Chase has added a mother, father, and two brothers to Jack's family and has Jack return home to be reunited with community and family. In "The Lion and the Unicorn," Jack has a mother and is not lazy in the earlier version, but the 1943 version does not mention a mother and Jack *is* lazy. For "Jack's Hunting Trip," Jack's family of father, mother, and two brothers in the earlier version is reduced to a father only in the later one. In addition, a tall tale about catching a lot of ducks is added to the later tale. Finally, in the earlier version of "Lucky Jack," Jack cuts off the king's head and marries his daughter; in the later version Jack does neither of these things.

Although the changes noted above are suggestive, the sample is too small to reveal any certain trends. Thus, I moved on to compare the traits in the tales Chase edited to those in tales collected from the same general area before his work or from an area beyond his influence.

Five collections formed the basis for this comparison. In 1923 Isabel Gordon Carter collected ten Jack tales from Jane Gentry in Hot Springs, North Carolina (Carter 1925). James Taylor Adams, with some assistance from James M. Hylton, collected twenty-eight Jack tales in 1941 and 1942. These tales came from a number of people in Wise County, Virginia, but the large majority point back to the Adams and Kilgore families, both of whom came to Virginia from an area in North Carolina not far from Beech Mountain (see Perdue 1987). The final three collections I analyze were compiled by Richard Chase: the six tales Chase collected between 1935 and 1939 and published in *Southern Folklore Quarterly*,[8] eighteen tales collected between 1935 and 1942 and published in *The Jack Tales* (1943);[9] and five tales collected between 1935 and 1942 and published in *American Folk Tales and Songs* (Chase 1956).[10] Appendix A presents a cross-correlation of the individual tales from these five sources, indicating the titles of tales included in each collection, as well as the tale types common to one or more collections.

In order to examine the character of Jack in the various collections of Jack tales, I constructed a list of eighty-four items (or categories) under nine general headings:

> Jack's Home Situation
> Jack's Personality Traits
> Jack's Skills or Professions

What Jack Does or Has Done to Him in the Tale
Helpers and Gifts
Jack's Opposition
How Jack Wins
Rewards
How the Tale Concludes

Appendix B shows the percentage of tales in each of the five collections listed above that contain each individual trait; this presentation suggests the prevalent narrative features within a collection and also allows for cross-comparison of specific traits in all five collections. In Appendix C, I have combined the pre-Chase tales (the collections of Carter and Adams) in one column and the three Chase collections in another, giving the number and percentage of tales in each of the two combined categories that contain the indicated trait. I believe that the figures in Appendix C provide the most meaningful data for discussion.

If we examine the more significant differences demonstrated by the comparisons in Appendix C, we find that Chase's tales put a considerably greater emphasis on home and family. In Chase's tales Jack more often has both a mother and father (34 percent of 29 tales vs. 8 percent of 38 tales). If a single parent is mentioned, it is much more likely to be a mother in Chase's collections (28 percent vs. 5 percent). The Chase tales give Jack two brothers more often than those collected by Carter and Adams (38 percent vs. 24 percent) and Jack is less often hired out or bound out (7 percent vs. 16 percent). Finally, Chase's Jack is much more apt to stay in or go back to his home community (an overwhelming 66 percent vs 8 percent).

Chase's personal history suggests some potential explanations for these differences. Various sources, including a 1984 interview with Chase, a transcription of a 1962 talk he gave,[11] and comments made by several anonymous informants, suggest that Richard Chase was a brilliant but difficult child. His father sent him to a special school in Tennessee for problem boys. Much later, after two years at Harvard, he says, "I had a spell of nervous . . . some kind of breakdown, you know—too much book-learning, and I came home and my dad was raising hell. . . . "

His father, a well-to-do nurseryman near Huntsville, Alabama, was a strict disciplinarian and believed in hard physical work. Richard did not live up to his expectations. Eventually, his father established a

This photograph of Richard Chase accompanied an
article about him that appeared in *The Charlotte Observer*, Jan. 1, 1978. See Peake Dana, "Special to *The
Observer*," Section C.

trust fund for his children and Chase, wherever he was living, received
a quarterly check. Some of those who knew him well said that the check
was "on condition that he not come home." In any event, he moved
around frequently and did not go back home until very late in his life
(see also Perdue 1987). It is not surprising that Richard Chase would
be concerned with "home" and, given his penchant for creative editing, it is no surprise that this concern is reflected in the tales.

In some cases, art follows life in Chase's tales: Jack is more than
twice as likely to be a braggart than he is in the Carter/Adams tales,
not inconsistent with Chase's well-known, sizeable ego. Chase's Jack
is more often betrayed by his brothers, reflecting perhaps Chase's
own troubled relationship with his siblings. But other changes occur

for which the connections are not so easily read. For example, Chase's Jack is more often a thief, more apt to dupe others, and is more than twice as likely to kill his opposition in the tales.

Chase was, of course, aware of the many changes that he made in the tales, and he saw a difference between what he called a "Scholars' Edition" and a "Popular Edition" of the Jack tales. In 1939, he wrote a letter to Nicholas Ray, WPA Recreation Division, indicating that the scholarly edition would include "full notes on sources and parallels of each separate tale; exact texts taken down phonographically, [both] from different informants, and from the same informant under varied circumstances and after certain intervals of time; and Notes on any dialectical points of importance brought out by [my proposed] project." Chase indicated that a popular edition would be a collation, but one done with "full knowledge of: Existing versions of the tales; knowledge of the lives and ways of the people who tell the tales; and knowledge of the background of each tale. . . . Obvious gaps in the existing versions should be filled in only where necessary points have been totally lost in oral tradition."[12]

For Chase, each tale existed—or had existed—in an ideal, complete form. His job, as he saw it, was to find as many versions of each tale as possible and collate something close to that ideal. He felt that he had an "instinct" for creating the "proper" collation from tale "fragments." The problem is that the "ideal" tale existed only in Chase's mind, and the tales he collated and published end up telling us more about Chase and his culture than that of the people from whom he gathered the tales.

In 1941, when Chase ostensibly was working on the proposed book of Wise County folklore, he had a romantic notion of what people there did and how they lived—or, at least, had lived—and he pursued that notion. In two letters to James Taylor Adams, he wrote that there was a main theme he wanted to present in the book and it should be stated by some citizen of the county who would say, "It's a lot better when folks get together to help one another out. That's the way people used to do and we ought to see if we can't do like that again." Chase wanted information on "house raisin's, log rollin's, corn shuckin's, apple peelin's, corn hoein's, stir offs, play parties," and other activities—many of which had died out before Chase reached the county. He wanted to use "actual facts" in the book but he stated,

> We may have to do a little faking now and then, but only when there is
> no other way to put across the thing that we want to do: to put the spirit
> of the traditions and all the really fine things in the County down in a
> good readable way. Life doesn't always happen like a story, and we have
> got to make a story out of all these materials.[13]

At the same time, Chase wrote to Eudora Ramsey Richardson, the
Virginia Writers' Project director and his supervisor in Richmond,
describing the stories he hoped to create:

> I'd like to make every single tale from Wise as good as, or better than,
> "Jack & Old Fire Dragaman"—which was edited from a number of oral
> variants heard around Beech Mountain:—a "creative synthesis" of 100%
> authentic source material.[14]

But Chase did not just utilize "authentic source material." He
reached into other traditions as well: "The wonderful curtain lines in
'Wicked John and the Devil' came from Zora Neale Hurston's *Mules
and Men,* a book of Negro folklore from Florida." In fact, the source
for the tale, Mrs. Jenning L. Yowell of Charlottesville, Virginia, had
called the protagonist of the tale "Wicked Jack." But Chase changed
"Jack" to "John" "to avoid confusion with the boy 'Jack' of *The Jack
Tales*" (Chase 1956:21). Put more bluntly, the change was made to
avoid confusion with Chase's characterization of Jack.

Chase admitted adding the words "of lies" to the phrase "singing
a bowl full" (Motif H1045) in "Fill, Bowl! Fill!" (1943, tale 10). And in
tale 18 in his 1943 collection, Chase had a blacksmith hammer little
devils to ashes on his anvil (similar to Motif K213). In the original
source Jack tied the Devils up for a couple of months and then released them to return home (Perdue 1987:113, 115).

Over the years, as Chase told the Jack tales he made further
changes to them. Children in his audiences would make suggestions—some of them quite good, he thought—and he would make
the changes in his future tellings. In "Jack in the Giants'
Newground"(1943, no. 1), Jack squeezes a rock held against a folded-
up apron filled with milk and "the milk commenced to dreen out."
A child suggested "spurted out" and Chase included that phrase in
his performances. He made so many such changes in his performances of the Jack tales that at one point he wanted to revise *The
Jack Tales*. He stated, "I've written Houghton Mifflin, 'Please let me

revise the Jack Tales. . . . ' They won't let me do it. I don't know what their excuse is, but someday, whether they let me or not, I'm gonna do it."[15] Chase never did revise his 1943 collection.

In Appalachia in 1870, local color writers discovered people whose lives and culture were somewhat different from their own. These writers

John Martin Kilgore and family. Mr. Kilgore narrated a number of Jack tales himself, and the Kilgore family, generally, is the source for many of the Wise County Jack tales. Photo from the James Taylor Adams Papers, John Cook Wyllie Library, Clinch Valley College, Wise, Virginia.

essentialized Appalachian culture and peoples, wrote about them for middle-class magazines, and began a process that continues today, a process that turned Appalachian people into the folk roots—the contemporary ancestors—of a presumed mainstream Anglo-Saxon America. Folk cultural productions had to be reshaped and repackaged—sanitized—so they could be sold to middle-class Americans who sought authentic expressions and representations of "their" national heritage. According to Becker, "With their specific histories replaced by generalizations, the folk and the past were domesticated—stripped of provocative differences and ready to carry new meanings assigned, this time, by their consumers" (1998:38).

This work was carried out by mission women, sociologists, folklorists, federal and state bureaucrats, corporate culture, craft revivalists, ballad hunters, cartoonists, and a host of other workers who used tradition—at least a particular idea of tradition—to sell various commodities from crafts to folksongs or to implement programs perceived as necessary (see also Bateaux 1990; McKay 1994; Shapiro 1972; Whisnant 1980, 1983).

The traditional artisans of the southern Appalachians saw their products appropriated first by retail craft centers and, ultimately, by factories that mass-produced replicas. Traditional singers of ballads and folksongs had their songs collected, published, and claimed as the property of urban, middle-class "revivalists." Through the work of Richard Chase and the storytelling revivalists who followed him, traditional Appalachian tellers of tales saw their stories change and become part of a global repertoire of American tales. Even Richard Chase, master agent of appropriation and changes that led eventually to the establishment of the Jonesborough Tennessee Storytelling Convention, complained bitterly that storytellers were stealing, telling, and ruining "his" Jack tales.[16]

Chase apparently did not appreciate the irony of his complaint, when he himself had felt as free to alter oral versions as the revivalist storytellers had felt licensed to alter his published texts. Change, of course, represents the dynamic face of traditional folklore expression. But as an academic folklorist, I am necessarily more concerned with change that occurs in the normal context of the traditional folklore performance than in change imposed from outside that context. In other words, changes made by Gaines Kilgore in repeated performances of telling the same Jack tale he learned from his grand-father are *not* equivalent to Richard Chase's conscious decision to add motifs from European sources or to add or delete material based on his own outside and elite aesthetic or intuitions.[17] The close comparisons offered here suggest that Chase did not simply present the tales told to him by Appalachian narrators; rather, through Richard Chase, Appalachian Jack became American Jack.

University of Virginia
Charlottesville

Appendix A: Cross-Correlation of Jack Tales in Selected Early Collections

CARTER (1925)	ADAMS (1941–42)*	CHASE (1937–41)**	CHASE (1943)	CHASE (1956)
1. Old Bluebeard ***	15A. Jack's Goose	5. Jack and the Fire Dragaman	12. Old Fire Dragaman	2. Jack and Old Tush
	15B. Suck All the Skin off Jack's Goose			
2. Lazy Jack and His Calf Skin			17. The Heifer Hide	4. Jack and the Talking Crow
3. Hardy Hardback			11. Hardy Hardhead	
4. Jack and the Fox			14. Cat 'n Mouse!	
5. The Enchanted Lady		6. Lucky Jack	10. Fill, Bowl! Fill!	
6. Jack the Giant Killer		1. Jack and the Giants	1. Jack in the Giants' Newground	
7. Sop, Doll, Sop			8. Sop Doll!	
8. Old Stiff Dick		2. The Lion and the Unicorn	6. Jack and the Varmints	
12. Jack and the North West Wind			5. Jack and the North West Wind	
13. Jack and the Beanstalk		4. Jack and the Bean Tree	3. Jack and the Bean Tree	
	1A. The Endless Tale			
	1B. The Longest Tale			
	1C. The Tale Without End			
	2. Fourteen			
	3A. Jack and the Bull		2. Jack and the Bull	5. Jack and Old Strongman
	3B. Jack and the Bull	2. Jack and the Bull		
	3C. Jack and the Bull			
	3D. Jack and the Bull			
	3E. Jack and the Bull			
	4. Jack and His Lump of Silver			
	5. Jack and Mossyfoot			
	6A. Jack and Old King Morock		15. Jack and King Marock	
	6B. Willie and the Devil			
	6C. Willie and the Devil			

7. Jack and the Beggar			
8. Jack and the Devil			
9. Jack and the Giant			
10. Jack and the Giant			
11. Jack Goes to Seek His Fortune			
12. Jack Goes to Seek His Fortune			
13. Jack and the Robbers	4. Jack and the Robbers		
14. Jack and the Woodchopper ****			
16. The Jack's Head			
17. Soldier Jack and the Magic Sack	18. Soldier Jack		
18. The Thieving Boy			
19. How Jack Got Tom to Do Will's Hard Work			
		16. Jack's Hunting Trips	
		7. Big Jack and Little Jack	
		9. Jack and the King's Girl	
3. Jack's Hunting Trip		13. Jack and the Doctor's Girl	
			3. Jack and the Old Rich Man
			1. Jack and the Witches

* Published in Perdue 1987.
** These tales were published in several issues of *Southern Folklore Quarterly* from 1937 to 1941.
*** Numbers immediately preceding tale titles refer to the numerical order of tales in each collection; letters indicate variants of a single tale type.
**** Adams (1941–42) tale no. 14 has elements of Carter (1925) no. 3, Chase (1943) no. 11, and Chase (1943) no. 9, but it is listed here as a separate tale.

Appendix B: Traits of Jack Tales in the Five Collections

Figures = Percent of Tales in the Collection with the Indicated Trait

Jack Tale Collection	Carter (1925) 10 tales	Chase (1937–41) 6 tales	Adams (1941-42)* 28 tales	Chase (1943) 18 tales	Chase (1956) 5 tales
Jack's Home Situation					
No mention of home or family	50%	17%	54%	28%	60%
Jack has father only	10		7	11	20
Jack has mother only		50	7	22	20
Jack has stepmother			7		
Jack has father and mother	10	33	7	44	
Jack raised by grandmother	10				
Jack has two brothers	40	33	18	44	20
Jack has one brother			4		
Family (or Jack) is poor	10	50	11	6	
Jack is orphaned	10		7		
Jack is hired out or bound out			21	6	20
Jack lives alone			4		20
Jack is married					20
Jack is mistreated at home	20		7	6	20
Jack begins tale on road alone			18	17	
Jack begins tale on road w/ company		7			
Jack's Personality Traits					
Jack is brave	30%	33%	21%	22%	20%
Jack is lazy	20		7	22	
Jack is kind		17	21	22	
Jack is clever	20	33	39	33	60
Jack is a braggart	30	50	7	28	20

Jack's Skills or Professions					
Jack is a gambler	10		14%	11%	11
Jack is a thief		33	4	11	20
What Jack Does or Has Done to Him					
Jack is betrayed by brothers	20%	17%		11%	11%
Jack's brothers try to kill him	10	17	7	11	20
Jack is asked/required to do difficult tasks	50	50	29	50	40
Jack gets duped	10		4	6	
Jack dupes others	30	33	25	33	60
Helpers and Gifts					
Help from old man	30%	17%		11%	33%
Help from old woman		17	17		
Help from young woman	10	17	14	11	20
Help from bull			18	6	
Help from animals			4	6	
Jack receives magic gift(s)	40	33	36	44	20
Jack receives advice	40	33	36	39	
Jack follows advice	30	33	36	33	
Jack does not follow advice	10			11	11
Jack receives direct help from helper	10	17	14	22	
Helper takes control			29	6	
Jack's Opposition					
Devil(s)	20%		14%	11	6%
Giant(s)	20	50	11		20
Witch(es)	10			17	20
King	10		18	11	

Appendix B: Traits of Jack Tales in the Five Collections (*continued*)

Jack Tale Collection	Carter (1925) 10 tales	Chase (1937–41) 6 tales	Adams (1941–42)* 28 tales	Chase (1943) 18 tales	Chase (1956) 5 tales
Jack's Opposition (*continued*)					
Brother(s)			4	6	20
Rich man		17		6	20
Old woman			18		
Old hairy or bearded man	10		11	11	40
Man and sons	10			6	
Misc. boys	10			6	
Robbers			11	6	
Animals	20	17		6	
Ghost			4		
Death			4	6	
No opposition		17	14		
How Jack Wins					
Jack kills directly	50%	67%	11%	39%	40%
Jack kills indirectly	20	33		22	40
Jack kills giant(s)	20	50	4	11	
Jack kills devil(s)				6	
Jack kills king	10				
Jack kills robber(s)			4		
Jack kills rich man	17			6	
Jack kills old man	10			11	20
Jack kills hairy or bearded man					20
Jack kills old woman			4	6	

	Col 1	Col 2	Col 3	Col 4	Col 5
Jack kills his brothers	10			6	40
Jack kills witch(es)	10			6	20
Jack kills animals	10				
Jack succeeds accidentally	20	33	7	11	
Helper wins for Jack			14	6	
Jack escapes	10	17	14		
Jack out-tricks opponent	20	33	39	28	40
Jack succeeds by accident and skill	10	17	4	11	40
Jack wins a contest	10		21		
Jack does not win			4		
Rewards					
Jack gets no reward	10%	33	25%	11%	20%
Girl	40	67	46	33	40
Money/jewels	70		32	44	60
Land and/or kingdom	10		18	17	40
Other property (clothes, horse, etc.)	20	33	18	39	60
Jack reunited with family	10		4	6	
How Tale Concludes					
Jack dies			7%		
Jack stays in or goes back to his community	20	67	4	72	40
Jack marries girl	40	33	29	22	40
Jack continues to seek fortune			11		

* Published in Perdue 1987

Appendix C: Traits of Jack Tales
(A Comparison of Richard Chase's Collections with Those of Other Early Collectors)
Figures = Number and Percent of Tales in the Collections with the Indicated Trait

Jack Tale Collections	❖ Carter (1925) + Adams (1941–42) * 38 tales		❖ Chase (1937–41, 1943, 1956) 29 tales	
Jack's Home Situation				
No mention of home or family	20 tales	53%	9 tales	31%
Jack has father only	3	8	3	10
Jack has mother only	2	5	8	28
Jack has stepmother	2	5		
Jack has father and mother	3	8	10	34
Jack raised by grandmother	1	3		
Jack has two brothers	9	24	11	38
Jack has one brother	1	3		
Family (or Jack) is poor	4	11	4	14
Jack is orphaned	3	8		
Jack is hired out or bound out	6	16	2	7
Jack lives alone	1	3	1	3
Jack is married			1	3
Jack mistreated at home	4	11	2	7
Jack begins tale on road alone	5	13	3	10
Jack begins tale on road w/ company	2	5		
Jack's Personality Traits				
Jack is brave	9 tales	24%	7 tales	24%
Jack is lazy	4	11	4	14
Jack is kind	6	16	5	17
Jack is clever	13	34	11	38
Jack is a braggart	5	13	9	31

Category / Item	Tales	%	Tales	%
Jack's Skills or Professions				
Jack is a gambler	4 tales	11%	2 tales	7%
Jack is a thief	2	5	5	17
What Jack Does or Has Done to Him				
Jack is betrayed by brothers	2 tales	5%	4 tales	14%
Jack's brothers try to kill him	3	8	4	14
Jack is asked/required to do difficult tasks	13	34	14	48
Jack gets duped	2	5	1	3
Jack dupes others	10	26	11	38
Helpers and Gifts				
Help from old man	6 tales	16%	7 tales	24%
Help from old woman			1	3
Help from young woman	4	11	4	14
Help from bull	5	13	1	3
Help from animals	1	3	1	3
Jack receives magic gift(s)	14	37	11	38
Jack receives advice	14	37	9	31
Jack follows advice	13	34	8	28
Jack does not follow advice	4	11	2	7
Jack receives direct help from helper	5	13	5	17
Helper takes control	8	21	1	3
Jack's Opposition				
Devil(s)	6 tales	16%	1 tale	3%
Giant(s)	5	13	6	21
Witch(es)	1	3	4	14
King	6	16	2	7

Appendix C: Traits of Jack Tales (*continued*)

Jack Tale Collections	❖ Carter (1925)	+ Adams (1941–42)* 38 tales		❖ Chase (1937–41, 1943, 1956) 29 tales	
Jack's Opposition (*continued*)					
Brother(s)		1	3	2	7
Rich man				3	10
Old woman		5	13		
Old hairy or bearded man		4	11	3	10
Man and sons		1	3	1	3
Misc. boys		1	3	1	3
Robbers		3	8	1	3
Animals		2	5	2	7
Ghost		1	3		
Death		1	3	1	3
No opposition		4	11	2	7
How Jack Wins					
Jack kills directly		8 tales	21%	13 tales	45%
Jack kills indirectly		2	5	8	28
Jack kills giant(s)		3	8	5	17
Jack kills devil(s)		1	3		
Jack kills king		1	3		
Jack kills robber(s)		1	3		
Jack kills rich man				2	7
Jack kills old man		1	3	3	10
Jack kills hairy or bearded man		1	3		
Jack kills old woman		1	3	1	3

	8 tales	21%	3 tales	10%
Jack kills his brothers	1	3	2	7
Jack kills witch(es)	1	3	2	7
Jack kills animals			1	3
Jack succeeds accidentally	4	11	4	14
Helper wins for Jack	4	11	1	3
Jack escapes	5	13	1	3
Jack out-tricks opponent	13	34	9	31
Jack succeeds by accident and skill	2	5	5	17
Jack wins a contest	7	18	2	7
Jack does not win	1	3		
Rewards	**8 tales**	**21%**	**3 tales**	**10%**
Jack gets no reward	17	45	10	34
Girl	16	42	15	52
Money/ jewels	5	13	5	17
Land and/or kingdom	7	18	12	41
Other property (clothes, horse, etc.)	1	3	1	3
Jack reunited with family			1	3
How Tale Concludes	**2 tales**	**5%**	**1 tale**	**3%**
Jack dies			19	66
Jack stays in or goes back to his community	3	8		
Jack marries girl	12	32	8	28
Jack continues to seek fortune	3	8		

* Published in Perdue 1987.

Notes

1. Letter, Richard Chase to James Taylor Adams, October 25, 1940. James Taylor Adams Papers, Archive, Box 47, John Cook Wyllie Library, Clinch Valley College, Wise, Virginia. For a more complete story of Chase's activities see Perdue 1987. For a discussion of Jack tales from a recently very active tradition see Halpert and Widdowson 1996; also Lovelace 1997 and this volume.

2. Letter, Richard Chase to James Taylor Adams, September 19, 1941. James Taylor Adams Papers, Box 47, John Cook Wyllie Library, Clinch Valley College, Wise, Virginia.

3. Letter, Richard Chase to Alan Lomax, May 5, 1942. Library of Congress, Archive of Folk Culture, Correspondence File under Richard Chase.

4. WPA Box 15, James Taylor Adams Papers, Archive, Box 47, John Cook Wyllie Library, Clinch Valley College, Wise, Virginia.

5. Chase either took this idea directly from Cecil Sharp or it was his idea and he validated it by quoting Sharp.

6. One tale survives from the Wise County collecting: a version of "Jack and the Bull," published in *Outwitting the Devil* (Perdue 1987) and reprinted here.

7. My initial efforts were spurred by the work of Sharon Smith, a student at the University of Virginia who wrote an honors thesis on the subject. The compilation of aspects—or traits—of Jack tales was greatly helped by the insights of Carl Lindahl of the University of Houston and Martin Lovelace of Memorial University, St. John's, Newfoundland. See Lindahl's very useful discussion "Jacks: The Name, the Tales, the American Traditions" (1994:xiii–xxxiv).

8. These six tales were collected from R. M. Ward, his brother Miles A. Ward, and Ben Hicks.

9. These much collated tales were collected by Chase from the Ward, Harmon, and Hicks families of Beech Creek, North Carolina; various people in Wise County, Virginia, and other localities in Virginia; with additions from tales collected by James Taylor Adams, James M. Hylton, and possibly others.

10. One tale was collected from seven individuals who lived in Eastern Kentucky, Southwestern Virginia, or near Beech Mountain, North Carolina. Another tale was told by two individuals in Wise County, Virginia, and one individual in Eastern Kentucky. One tale was copied by Anna Presnell from Frank Profitt's copy, which he, in turn had written from the telling of his father Wiley Profitt and published in the appendix to *The Jack Tales*. One tale was cited only as a "Virginia version," and one tale was attributed to "Tom Hunt"—the nom de plume of Richard Chase.

11 The interview was conducted on November 8, 1984 by Nancy J. Martin-Perdue and me. The transcript of the 1962 talk can be found in the Beulah Campbell Collection, Appalachian Culture Museum, Appalachian State University, Boone, North Carolina.

12. From a two-page typescript, undated but accompanied by a letter from Chase to Nicholas Ray, Recreation Division, W.P.A., March 19, 1939. In National Archive, RG 69, 651.36 Va.

13. Two letters from Chase to James Taylor Adams, September 19, 1941, and

September 27, 1941, James Taylor Adams Papers, Archive, Box 47, John Cook Wyllie Library, Clinch Valley College, Wise, Virginia.

14. Letter from Richard Chase to Eudora Ramsey Richardson, November 9, 1941, Library of Virginia, WPA-VWP collection, Box 256, Folder 8.

15. Chase talked about the changes in "Jack in the Giants' Newground" in our interview with him in 1984. The quote about Houghton Mifflin is from his 1962 talk, cited in note 11 above.

16. Chase made this complaint during the interview my wife and I conducted with him on November 8, 1984.

17. My comments on "change" here are essentially what I said in *Outwitting the Devil* (1987:92). For one example of changes beyond even Chase's fantasy, see Haley 1992. For versions of Jack tales from a contemporary teller who claims descent from the tradition, see Davis 1992.

References Cited

Bateaux, Allen
1990   *The Invention of Appalachia.* Tucson: University of Arizona Press.
Becker, Jane S.
1998   *Selling Tradition: Appalachia and the Construction of an American Folk, 1930–1940.* Chapel Hill: University of North Carolina Press.
Carter, Isabel Gordon
1925   "Mountain White Folk-Lore: Tales from the Southern Blue Ridge." *Journal of American Folklore* 38/149:340–74.
Chase, Richard
1937a "Jack and the Giants." *Southern Folklore Quarterly* 1/1:35–41.
1937b "The Lion and the Unicorn." *Southern Folklore Quarterly* 1/4:15–19.
1938a "Jack's Hunting Trip." *Southern Folklore Quarterly* 2/3:145–48.
1938b "Jack and the Bean Tree." *Southern Folklore Quarterly* 2/4:100–02.
1939a "Lucky Jack." *Southern Folklore Quarterly* 3/1:21–24.
1939b "The Origin of 'The Jack Tales.'" *Southern Folklore Quarterly* 3/2:187–91.
1941   "Jack and the Fire Dragaman." *Southern Folklore Quarterly* 5/3:151–55.
1943   *The Jack Tales.* Cambridge, Mass.: Houghton Mifflin Company.
1948   *Grandfather Tales.* Cambridge, Mass.: Houghton Mifflin Company.
1956   *American Folk Tales and Songs: and other Examples of English American Tradition as Preserved in the Appalachian Mountains and Elsewhere in the United States.* New York: New American Library.
1962   Transcript of a talk by Richard Chase, Beulah Campbell Collection, Appalachian Culture Museum, Appalachian State University, Boone, North Carolina.
Davis, Donald
1992   *Jack Always Seeks His Fortune: Authentic Appalachian Jack Tales.* Little Rock, Ark.: August House.
Haley, Gail E.
1992   *Mountain Jack Tales.* New York: Dutton Children's Books.

Halpert, Herbert, and J. D. A. Widdowson
1996 *Folktales of Newfoundland.* New York: Garland Publishing, Inc.
Karpeles, Maud, ed.
1932 *English Folk Songs from the Southern Appalachians,* Collected by Cecil J. Sharp. London: Oxford University Press.
Lindahl, Carl
1994. "Jacks: the Name, the Tales, the American Traditions." In *Jack in Two Worlds: Contemporary North American Tales and Their Tellers,* ed. William Bernard McCarthy, xiii–xxxiv. Chapel Hill: University of North Carolina Press.
Lovelace, Martin
1997 "Jack and His Masters." Paper presented at American Magic: The Fates of Oral Fiction in the New World. A Conference on Folktales and Their Cultural Contexts. University of Houston, Houston, Texas.
Martin-Perdue, Nancy J., and Charles L. Perdue
1996 *Talk About Trouble: A New Deal Portrait of Virginians in the Great Depression.* Chapel Hill: University of North Carolina Press.
McCarthy, William Bernard, ed.
1994 *Jack in Two Worlds: Contemporary North American Tales and Their Tellers.* Chapel Hill: University of North Carolina Press.
McKay, Ian
1994 *The Quest of the Folk: Antimodernism and Cultural Selection in Twentieth - Century Nova Scotia.* Montreal: McGill-Queens University Press.
Oxford, Cheryl
1994 "The Storyteller as Curator: Marshall Ward." In *Jack in Two Worlds: Contemporary North American Tales and Their Tellers,* ed. William Bernard McCarthy, 56–92. Chapel Hill: University of North Carolina Press.
Perdue, Charles L., Jr.
1987 *Outwitting the Devil: Jack Tales from Wise County Virginia.* Santa Fe: Ancient City Press.
Shapiro, Henry D.
1978 *Appalachia on Our Mind: The Southern Mountains and Mountaineers in the American Consciousness, 1870–1920.* Chapel Hill: University of North Carolina Press.
Whisnant, David E.
1980 *Modernizing the Mountaineer.* New York: Burt Franklin.
1983 *All That is Native and Fine: The Politics of Culture in an American Region.* Chapel Hill: University of North Carolina Press.

A Model of Appropriate Behavior? "The Ship That Sailed on Land and Water"

Alice Lannon (b. 1927) of Placentia, Newfoundland, has three magic tales, among many other narratives, in her active repertoire. In 1991 she published them in *Fables, Fairies and Folklore of Newfoundland* (St. John's: Jesperson Press), a book she wrote with her brother, Michael McCarthy. There she notes that the three tales have been passed down in her family, entirely by oral transmission, over some 150 years. Women were the sole tradition bearers, in that Alice learned them from her grandmother, Mary Strang McCarthy, who came to live with them when Alice was thirteen. Mary Strang had them from her mother's sister, Aunt Ellen Flanagan; they were, as the names suggest, of Irish descent. When Barbara Rieti and I visited Alice in June 1999 to videotape her narration of the three tales, she told us of using them as bedtime stories for her children and as distractions for her daughters while she brushed tangles from their hair. Although the principal context for her storytelling was (and remains) within her family, she once told "The Ship That Sailed on Land and Water" to an airline pilot while she was flying to Australia; it seemed appropriate. Alice Lannon is a superb narrator and I am deeply grateful for the opportunity to record this version of one of her tales.

The tale published here—evidence that the magic tale is not yet gone from Newfoundland oral tradition—is an example of "The Land and Water Ship" (AT 513B), prefaced by "Squeezing the (Supposed) Stone" (AT 1060) and "Eating Contest" (AT 1080). In many ways, it is a male-centered tale. Jack's boast that he can do "anything a good strong man can do" typifies the aggressive self-confidence the tales seem to recommend as a model of how working men should be when facing employers (see "Jack and His Masters," this volume). Alice's two other tales are female-centered, following the fortunes of poor young girls, but here she takes on a masculine tale and gives it a feminine slant. Jack is good to his mother, and this saves his life when he uses the leather bag she gives him—containing a half cake *with her blessing*—in a ruse to defeat the giant. A second old woman, the stick-gatherer Jack befriends, gives him the cheese curds that the giant mistakes for stones. The giant's hyper-masculine display of strength leads to his own undoing: "If you can do it, so can I!" the giant says, as he tries to squeeze water from rocks and stabs himself in the stomach, as he thinks he has seen Jack do. The giant's over-competitiveness might be read as a shrewd dig at overbearing male braggarts. At the end of the tale Jack fetches his mother before his wedding takes place, and she in turn "lived to see the grandchildren grow up." It is thus made quite clear that Jack's success depends not on his own merit, but rather on his kindness to elders and particularly to women.

Barbara Rieti and I recorded the "The Ship That Sailed on Land and Water" at Placentia, Newfoundland, on June 26, 1999. The transcription is mine.

Martin Lovelace
Memorial University of Newfoundland

"The Ship That Sailed on Land and Water"*
as told by Alice Lannon, June 26, 1999

So, once upon a time in a far away land, there was three brothers, Jack, Bill, and Tom. They lived with their mother, and their father was dead, and times were poor. And this year it had been an exceptionally poor year, the crops had failed, and food was getting scarce.

So one night as they sat around the table, discussing what they were going to do, the oldest fellow, Tom, said "Mom, I think I'll go seek my fortune," and uh he said "Bake me a cake in the ashes before the crow flies over the corner of the house."

So she got up the next morning and baked the cake and she called out, "Tom, Tom, the cake be ready"—now that's what Grandmother used to say, I guess that was the terms in the story, "cake be ready."

And he came down and had his meager breakfast and she packed up the cake for 'n, and as she was packing it up she said "Will you have the half of it with my blessing, or the whole of it with my curse?"

And he said, "The whole of it with your curse is little enough for me!"

"Oh Tom," she said, "I was hoping you'd want my blessing," but she gave it to him anyhow—

And he started out, put his pack on his back, and he went down the lane and down the . . . up the road, and across the hill, down by a river. And he was walking and it was around noon, he looked up and the sun was overhead, so he figured it was time for lunch. He set down by the riverbank, and he dipped up a little uh mug of water that he have to drink with his lunch, and as he set down a little old man came out of the woods and said "Can I pick up the crumbs when you're through?"

* For an explanation of the transcription conventions used here, see note 3, p.168.

"Pick up the crumbs!" he said, "I'll give you a kick and put you on the other side of the river! Go away and stop tormentin' me."

And the little old man shook his head, and said "I'm afraid you'll come to a bad end."

And when Tom went to go get a drink of water, another drink, the little old man took out a stick and stirred it up and turned all muddy and bloody and he couldn't get any more water. And he disappeared in the woods, so Tom went on and he wandered all day and just before nightfall he came to a big farm and, was a gate there and the sign said "Man wanted."

So he wandered up to the door, when he knocked on the door a big old giant fellow opened the door, *[angrily]* "What do **you** want?

He said, "You, you're looking for a **man**," he said, "and I'm looking for **work**."

And he said uh, "And what can **you** do?" the old giant said.

He said, "Anything a good strong man can do."

"Well," he said, "you see that uh spot of woods is over there?" he said, "I want all that cut down, uh sawed up, and stacked up," he said, "between sunrise and sunset."

And Tom said "Well, where do I sleep?"

"In the barn," he said. "In the hay(out) part."

And old Tom was so tired he stumbled down and fell into the hay and went to sleep.

In the morning a servant called him, no such thing as **breakfast** or anything, so Tom went to uh—took the axe and the saw and he went over to the wood lot and start cutting and sawing, and he worked so hard and b'y he was hungry, lunch time came, no lunch, and he worked and about three o'clock, he had a lot of the wood done, but he was so tired and weak from the hunger he sat down.

And the old giant came along: "Sittin' down on the job! Off with his head and put it on a spear, to show others what laziness gets ya." So, that was the end of poor Tom.

And time passed, and they hadn't had word, so uh Jack and Bill and his mother one night were talking about it, wondering what happened to him, and Bill said, "I think **I'll** go seek my fortune."

So the same thing, he said to his mother "Bake me a cake in the ashes before the crow flies over the corner of the house." And she got up and did as she was bid and the next morning—she called out, uh, "Bill, Bill, the cake be ready!"

Bill came down and ate his meager breakfast, (there was) food was getting **scarcer**, and she was wrapped up the cake for him, and she said "Will you have the half of it with my blessing or the whole of it with my curse?"

"The whole of it with your curse is little enough for **me!**"

And she shook her head, she said "I thought you'd want my blessing." But she gave it to him anyway.

And off he went, and he followed the same trail as his brother, and he came to the same little spot by the river at noon time, and when he took out his lunch the little old man came out and asked the same **question**: "Can I pick up the crumbs?"

And he said the same thing: "I'll give ye a kick and put ya on th' other side of the river!"

"You'll be sorry," he said, "you'll come to a bad end."

And he did the same, when when uh Bill went below to get more water, he stirred it up and 'twas mud, and blood, and all, not fit to **drink**. So, he, Bill was kind of mad, but the little man disappeared into the **woods**.

And he came, he wandered until nightfall, came to the same sign, "Man wanted," and went up to the door, same old giant opened the door, and uh he said "What do **you** want?"

He said "I'm lookin' for **work**, you said, your sign says you want a **man**."

"What can **you** do?"

"Anything a good strong **man** can do."

He said, "You see that field of corn over there?" he said. "I want that **cut** and tied up," he said, "and uh—in **bundles**. (Now) it has to be done between uh, sun up and sun set."

And uh Bill figured "Well, I guess I can do that, and where do I sleep?"

"In the barn, with the hay."

And he was so hungry, he wished he had something to eat but he was afraid to **ask**.

So he went down to the barn, and went to sleep, and next morning servant called him and up he got, and he went out and he was cutting the corn, and tyin' it up in bundles and noontime came, nothing to eat, and he was even thirsty, was no **water** around, and the sun was so hot, and he was really overcome, so **he** set down by a, a tree stump, and fell asleep.

And the old giant came along: "Off with his head!" Put his head on a spear. And that was the end of poor Bill—

Time passed, and the mother and Jack wondered what happened to the two boys, so Jack said "I think I'll go seek my **fortune**. Bake me a cake in the ashes before the crow flies over the corner of the house." And the mother said "I hate to see you go, Jack, you're a good worker, and a good boy."

So the next morning, when he went down for his breakfast, she uh, was wrapping up the cake, and she said "Will you have the half of it with my blessing, or the whole of it with my curse?"

"Oh Mom," he said, "the half of it with your blessing for sure."

And she said "I was only testin' ya, take it all."

"Oh no," he said, "you keep some for yourself." He said "A **half** is enough for **me**."

But she insisted, and she gave him a leather **bag**, and he put the cake in a bag, and hung it inside his shirt, round his neck inside his shirt.

So, when he followed the same trail as his brothers, and when he came to the little brook, uh, where the grassy spot was, he set down to have his **lunch**, and the little old man came out of the woods, and said "Can I pick up the **crumbs**?"

And Jack said, uh, "Pick up the **crumbs**?" He said, "Here, come, I'll **share** with ya!" And he gave him a piece of his cake.

And when Jack went to dip up his, drop of water, the little old man put the stick down and here it turned into fine wine. He had a, a lovely snack.

And he said to him, he said "Jack," he said, "you're a fine man." He said "You'll go far in life." He said "I have a uh, I know a king, in a far away kingdom, who has uhm a **daughter** that he's looking for a **husband** for, and" he said, "you'd make her a good husband."

So Jack laughed at that, he said "How would I get **there**?"

"Well, now," he said, "I could build you a ship that'll sail over land and water."

And Jack thought it was the railings of a senile old man, so he just laughed at him, and thanked him, and he went on his way.

And he said "Now I . . . " the little old man called out, "Now remember, if you want that favor, come back to me."

So Jack went to the same route as the brothers, and came to the same gate with the sign "Man wanted," and he went up and he knocked on the door, and the, the giant said, uh, "What do **you** want?"

"I'm looking for work and you, your sign says you need a man."

"What can you do?"

"Anything a good strong man can do."

And he said, "I have a big field of hay over here," he said, "I want it cut, and put in piles." He said, "It has to be done between uh sun up and sun set."

And Jack said, "I been traveling all day and I'm hungry," he said, "can I get something to eat?"

The old giant thought, "Ah, he's a smart guy!" So he said, "Go to the, the cook house," he said, "and the cook'll give you a meal."

So Jack had a good meal, and he came out and he washed his face and hands at the pump where the big trough was for the cattle to get water, and then he went in, down, fell into the hay and went to sleep.

So when he was called the next morning to go to work, it wasn't quite sun up so he went back to the cook house and demanded breakfast. He wasn't going to work on an empty stomach! And he went and the old giant thought "I'll have to do something to him, 'cause he's too smart!"

And he cut the hay and he had it done long, long before uh sun down, 'twas all finished. And he went back to the cook house and got his supper.

And the, the old giant said, "Now I have another job for you to-morrow." He said uh "The grass is getting eaten here," he said, "in this pasture," he said, "I have twelve head of cattle, and I want you to take 'em over," he said, "see that pasture over there, on the other side of the river. Well," he said, "you can't get their **hooves** wet."

And uh Jack decided that uh, well, he sized up the river and he found a narrow spot and he put some rocks and build up with . . . and then he found some planks, and he laid the planks across, and he made a bridge, he drove his, the cows across, there was no, the old giant was watchin', he said, "He's a smart cookie! There's no use not to . . . they're not going to get their feet wet."

So when he got up to the other side, the cattle were glad to be in the new, rich pasture, so they start eating, and this little old woman she had a, trying to put a bundle of sticks on her back, and Jack said to her, "Here, let me help you," he said. "I'll take it for you, where do you live?" "Over under the hill," she said, "in that little cottage."

So, the cows were eating the grass, so Jack took the, her bundle of wood and brought it over and right to her door. She wanted him to come in and have something to eat, and he said "Oh, uh, no," he said, "I had a good breakfast," he said, uh, "I can't, I haven't got the time, now."

"But" she said, "here, here's some uh **curds**," she said. "A little bundle of curds," she said, "take it." And she said, "And you'll have a snack on it," so he put it in his pocket.

And he wasn't long there when the old giant came out, and . . . **worst** than the one that **he** was working for.

"**Who told you to come on my pasture?**"

"**Your** pasture?" says Jack. "My master said 'twas his."

He said "He's always tryin' to best me." He said, "Do you know," he said, "that I could grind you up," he said, "just like this," and he scooped up the rocks and he ground them to fine sand, and [the fella] . . . and Jack said, uh, "Can you squeeze water out of 'em?" He *[Jack]* said, "I'll try."

So Jack pretended he scooped up the rocks, he took the curds in his hand, and when he squeezed the the [along with] the rocks here the whey ran out, and the old giant was vicious.

"If you can do it, so can I!" He was going around, grabbin' up the rocks, squeezing 'em, no water! "Ye've bested me at that," he said. "So now," he said, "we're going to have a contest." He said "I have some soup cooking," he said, "and we're going to have uh, see who can drink the most."

And Jack thought to himself, "Huh, you know who's going to drink the **most**, old giant. I can't hold soup like that."

So when he went in the old giant dished up the great big bowl of soup, and it was good, Jack enjoyed it, but the old, he was so busy, drinking the soup hisself, that every time he filled Jack's bowl, Jack tipped it into the leather bag he had around his neck.

And uh the old giant said, "Well I can't believe," he said, "that you've beat me drinking soup. And" he said, "if you beat me at one more thing," he said, "you can have my, have this castle, the farm, the servants, everything that's here'll be yours. Including," he said, "money. Bags of money," he said, "in the store room."

And Jack thought about it and he said uh . . . "You said you could do anything I can do. Have you got a sharp **knife?**"

"Yes," he said, and he gave him a big butcher knife.

"Well," Jack said, "we better go **outside.**"

And he dragged the knife right into the leather bag and all the soup spilled out.

And the old giant was so mad *[spoken quickly]* "If you can do it, so can I!" And he dragged the knife through his stomach and fell down dead! *[laughing]* So the servants buried him, and they were all so glad, because he was a wicked old giant!

Now, Jack owned the place. So he started thinking about it and he said, "I'll go back to the little old man, [and ask] him about his ship that could sail over land and water."

And the little old man was delighted to see him, and he went down and he picked up some wire, some sticks, and old things around, a bit of canvas, and before long, there was the oddest looking uh contraption that Jack had ever seen. It wasn't like a ship, and he told him that there was special stuff he had in a can that would make it go. And he said, told him how to work it, and he said uh "You skim over the tree tops," and how to come down and land, and he showed Jack everything. "So now," he said, "you're ready to go seek your fortune, and uh the princess's hand in marriage. But," he said, "you'll need a crew. So," he said, "as you're going along," he said, "and you see someone walking, call out, and see what, if they're looking for work. And if they are," he said, "lower down the bucket and take 'em on board."

So the first fella that Jack was, flied over a roadway, and this man was walking along, and Jack called out "What are ya doin'?"

"I'm lookin' for work," he says.

So Jack said, "Climb in the bucket." Hauled him up. And uh, "What can you do?"

"Anything a good strong man can do, but I can **run** faster than anyone else in the world. My name is Run-fast."

So, he was hired.

And then he went along, there was another fella, pulled him up, he was **Shoot-all**. He could shoot better than anyone in the world. Then there was **See**-all, he could **see** better than anyone else in the world, his name was See-all, and Shoot-all, and Run-fast. And then there was a fella, he was called, he was **Never-be-warm**. Now, he never got warm in his life, his aim was some time to be warm. He was always cold. And, Jack didn't know what good he'd be, but he hired him, and uh, there was a fella could see-all, he could see better than anyone else, and Tear-all, he could tear up trees, by the roots, and swing 'em around, and oh he had wonderful fun at that. And the last fella he came to was Hard-ass. He could slide down mountains, and level down *[laughing]* the hills!

So, Jack had 'em all aboard. Now he's took off for the kingdom. Where the king's, was offering his, looking for a husband for his **daughter**. So, uh, Jack, when he went up to the castle he saw this pretty girl sittin' by the window. And he said "I hope she's the one that he's lookin' for a **husband** for!" And she saw Jack and she said "I hope he's the fella my father picks for **me**!"

So the king [said] there was so many things that had to be done. Jack, or one of his crew, had to do it before he could have the . . . girl's hand in marriage. The first one was, he had a king, a friend, who lived on the other side of the world. And he, Jack had to have someone that could run to the other side of the world and come back, with the answer, between sun up and sunset.

And he came back to the [boat], to the ship, and he was feelin' pretty down, "That's impossible." And Run-fast said, "That's the job for me!"

So the next morning, the king, they went up to the castle, just before sun up, the king gave 'em a note. And Run-fast shot off like a, like little *[laughs]* like a shot out of a gun, he was gone, they couldn't see him. And he said to Jack, he said, "I'll be back before three o'clock," he said. "Don't worry about that."

And, anyhow, three o'clock came, no sign of Run-fast. Jack and his crew were gettin' worried. So Hear-all, I don't know if I mentioned him, he put his ear to the ground and he could hear someone snoring. He said, "I believe Run-fast fell asleep." And uh, . . . See-all went up to the hill and climbed a tree, and he could see Run-fast asleep, with a sleepy-pin in his ear! There was an old witch, she pretended that she wanted Jack *[Run-fast]* to help her put a bundle on her back, and when he stooped down to pick it up she stuck a sleepy-pin in his ear and he fell asleep.

So Shoot-all said, "Well, if See-all can point the gun, I'll pull the trigger," and they shot the sleepy-pin out of his ear. And up jumped Run-fast and he was home in no time, with the, the answer.

So that was once, and then the King said, uh, he had a, there was a big hill up there, with a forest, and he wanted all those trees pulled up, cleared off, he wanted the ground cleared. And Tear-all said "That's the job for me!" So Tear-all had a wonderful time! He went up and just as the sun was comin' up he was pullin' up big trees by their roots and throwing 'em in a pile!

And the, the king said, uhm, "I want," he said, "all those trees set fire, and someone got to stay in the middle of 'em while they're being burnt." And Jack thought, "Well, no one can do that!" Never-be-warm said, "That's the job for me! I might get warm once in my life!"

So anyhow, that night when they had all the trees piled, Never-be-warm crawled in through the hole and the old king set fire to it. And poor Jack walked away, he he thought he'd, he'd never see him again, he thought he was going to be burnt to a cinder. But anyhow when they used to look in they could see Never-be-warm sitting in the flames, big grin on his face!

And uh, when it came daylight, the woods all burnt down, and uh, uh they pulled uh, he was pullin' a few coals around him tryin' to get warm, and when the king said to him, you know, "How come you didn't burn?" "Well," he said, "I was disappointed. I thought," he said, "I was going to get warm for once in me life!" So that was Never-be-warm. So he had that done.

Then there was uh, he wanted uh, he had a cellar full of **wine**, and he said uh, he had, wanted someone to drink all that wine, and rum, and whisky, whatever was there, and not get drunk. So Drink-all was one of the crew, and Drink-all said "That's the job for me." And all night he was down in the cellar, and the next morning when uh Jack and the king went to check, he was tipping up the cask, draining it out, trying to get the last of it. And he was sober as if he had only been drinking water.

So then the, the mountain had to be leveled down. He wanted this mountain leveled down. And Hard-ass said "That's the job for me!" And he ran up the hill and he used to **slide** down, and all the ground and everything would come with him, and then he'd scoot right along on his bum and level it off, 'twas big as a football field, level as [anything] *[laughing]*.

So the king said "Well, you've met all my requirements, so now you can have my daughter's hand in marriage." The princess was delighted, Jack was delighted, and he *[the King]* said, "And I'll give you a castle." And Jack said, "I don't need a castle. I have my own place. But first," he said, "I got to go get my mother, and bring her with me."

So, Jack got in his ship that could sail over land and water, and picked up his mother, and came back to the king's castle, they had a big wedding, and then Jack and his bride moved back to his pla—the old giant's place that he had won from him, and they had uh a family of children, and his mother lived to see the grandchildren grow up, and they all lived happily ever after! *[laughs]*

Martin Lovelace

Jack and His Masters: Real Worlds and Tale Worlds in Newfoundland Folktales

> If the crew are to be carried away to an unbeknown place, they all go
> below to a man, for *Jack's as good as his master* when it comes to his hav-
> ing to do something which he didn't agree for.[1]

THE PUBLICATION IN 1996 of Herbert Halpert and John Widdowson's
Folktales of Newfoundland[2] has provided a huge new corpus of North
American versions of international magic tales. This magisterial collection opens many opportunities for comparison and speculation, particularly in light of Bengt Holbek's arguments, in his 1987 work *Interpretation of Fairytales,* that Märchen were symbolic representations of
common conflicts, drives, and aspirations in everyday peasant life. There
are many ways these tales can be read now that, regrettably, they are
rarely told: here I emphasize their presentation of consistent advice,
mainly to young men, about ways to conduct themselves in seeking
and keeping work. While realizing that this is only one facet of these
marvelously complex narratives, I intend to focus on these Newfoundland tales as deliberate, albeit sometimes coded, representations of the
"master and man" employment relationship. They are lessons in life as
seen from the perspective of a subordinated social class.

Newfoundland is a hard luck place. Current unemployment lev-
els are among the highest in North America. The great cod fisheries
of the Grand Banks attracted European exploitation from the fifteenth
century onward, and in the eighteenth and nineteenth centuries particularly there was permanent settlement, especially from the west of
England, south-east Ireland, western France, and the Channel Islands.
In the last ten years, an industrialized fishery, Canadian and international, has fished the cod to the point of extinction. The small outport
communities in which these tales were told as a regular entertainment

into the 1950s and collected as a fading tradition in the 1960s and
1970s have in some cases been completely abandoned, and more will
share this fate.

But work was never constant in Newfoundland. Unlike the nine-
teenth-century Danish peasants whose tales were recorded by Evald
Tang Kristensen and interpreted by Bengt Holbek (1987), these Newfoundland young men were not waiting to inherit small farms that
would be their "kingdoms." Rather, they were obliged to live by occupational pluralism. Besides fishing—often with family members—they
might cobble together an income by working in the woods in the
winter, going to the ice for seals in the spring, and building wharves,
roads or other projects when a politician needed votes. Negotiating
for work was a common and continuing experience. The storytellers
who gave their tales to Halpert and Widdowson had all experienced
the Depression of the 1930s, and there are plenty of asides about
poverty in the tellers' own times, as well as in the world of the tales, to
show that they identified strongly with this "given" feature of the magic
tale: the search by the poor hero for work.

The perception that a "real world" might lie not far beneath the
magical surface of the Märchen is, of course, far from new. Lutz Röhrich
has said that "investigation of the folktale's relationship to
reality . . . drives at the genre's essence" (1991:1); Satu Apo has examined social-historical reality in Finnish magic tales (1995:199–224). In
Newfoundland, Gerald Thomas has begun to issue a series of exciting
and persuasive analyses of meaning in tales, taking a "post-Holbekian
perspective" to Märchen in his extensive narrative collections from
French-speaking communities of the Port-au-Port peninsula (1997,
1999). Gyula Ortutay's 1941 essay on the Hungarian storyteller Mihály
Fedics, however, remains one of the most cogent statements about the
potential relationship between tale worlds and real worlds. He suggests that Märchen heroes are characterized by "a rebellious desire
for the re-creation of the world and for heroic adventure, combined
with the serf's fear and religious humility in the face of the realm of
secrets and powers. That is how the hero of a tale faces valiantly what
is impossible to accomplish, how he always abides by the law and obeys
strict orders and observes the inviolable laws that are met with even
in tales" (Ortutay 1972:253). In Ortutay's view, it is a peasant's forti-
tude in adversity that appears in magic tales, while the autocratic ogres

and task setters in them are reflections of the human masters who ruled over peasants in daily life. Linda Dégh's *Folktales and Society* and her essay "The Peasant Element in the Hungarian and East European Magic Tale" also attend to the interrelationship between real world and tale world (1969, 1981).

A key phrase for this essay, however, came as a result of many summer evenings watching my son play peewee baseball in Newfoundland. Whenever a particularly good play was made, coaches and teammates would yell "How to *beee!*" It came to me that Newfoundland magic tales might similarly be expressions of a "way to be" addressed by older men to younger men, and boys in particular, and that just as the baseball cheer evaluates competent performance, so these tales depict how to be a competent man in getting work, how to deal with employers and other adversaries, whom to trust, and how to present oneself in various areas of life, including courtship. I orient my analysis toward what Holbek calls "male-centered" tales, rather than the female-centered tales that are equally important in forming the genre as a whole, because the majority of the tales in *Folktales of Newfoundland are* male-centered: the narrators are male and they identify with their protagonist, Jack. This was not a choice made by the two fieldworkers, but rather a result of what Barbara Rieti, who has done a great deal of fieldwork in rural Newfoundland, describes as a consequence of being sent along a male network. Even though she would like to have recorded more female narrators it was predominantly men to whom she was directed: "a man tends to send one on to another man" (Rieti 1991:214). Marie-Annick Desplanques (1985) and Gerald Thomas (1983, 1993) have recorded more female storytellers, especially in what Thomas has called the "private tradition" of household storytelling by women, but *Folktales of Newfoundland* contains only one magic tale by a woman. As a whole the collection is primarily representative of the male, public, storytelling tradition.

A male narrator does not preclude the inclusion of strong female characters, however. It is in fact striking that, as Holbek similarly argues for Danish peasant tales, women in the majority of the Newfoundland tales are portrayed as equal, or even dominant, partners in bringing about the success of the love relationship. (The same might well be observed about the Newfoundland folksong corpus.) This would mirror social reality in a culture in which the woman was responsible for more than half of the many tasks necessary for success in the family fishery (Murray 1979). Such impressions about the respective roles of men and women, as depicted in Halpert and Widdowson's collection, may be given more substance through the structural analysis that follows.

A Structural Analysis

Although *Folktales of Newfoundland* contains what W. F. H. Nicolaisen has called a "lavish, almost festive, scholarly apparatus" (1997:94), Halpert and Widdowson did not include a structural analysis as part of their interpretive work. What follows is an attempt at such an analysis in order to reflect and explore the weight placed on work in these tales. I find six tale-roles:

1. the hero
2. the employer
3. the adversary
4. the donor
5. the helper
6. the partner

By putting the majority of the magic tales in the collection through this schema I discovered the following tendencies:

1. The hero is usually named Jack, the youngest of three brothers, a poor boy though sometimes a king's son; as Widdowson notes, whether king's son or poor boy, Jack acts the same.
2. Employers are giants (1 instance), magicians (2), kings (5), and farmers (5).
3. Adversaries (listing only those that appear more than twice) are magicians (3), giants (5), old women (6), treacherous brothers (6), and treacherous sea captains (8).
4. Donors are birds (2), giants (2), grateful dead men (including one spirit) (3), old women (4), and old men (16). (The tale role of donor, as with helper below, follows Propp [1968].)
5. Helpers are a dog, a fish, a bull, and an old woman (1 each); birds, grateful dead men, and six fools (2 each).
6. Partners are all unmarried young women who fall in love with the hero; in seven of twenty-two tales where this role occurs the woman is a princess and in seven others she is an ogre's daughter.

My analysis here is rough and ready, but it is more than impressionistic. Certain traits stand out: first, in a culture that sees itself as oriented to the sea there is a remarkable number of references to farmers. Magicians, kings, and farmers all impose tasks, often on pain of death. Among adversaries, old women score high; this may reflect a traditional suspicion of witches, though men can also be called witches in the tales and in real life. Brothers are treacherous, which is interesting given that men in Newfoundland often work with their brothers. In a bit of metacommentary during a tale, one teller notes, "You can't trust your brother" (Halpert and Widdowson 1996:26). Sea captains are not presented as employers, nor as the respected figures they are in real life, but as abductors of boys and young women. The tales suggest that it is wise to respect the dead—"the grateful dead man" is a fairly common motif—but they particularly imply that old people should be honored and treated with charity and that old men give good advice.

The Tale Occasions

Tales were told to different kinds of audiences, in several typical contexts, on various kinds of occasion. House-visits, especially in winter, involved the nuclear family and neighbors, who were also often relatives. In a 1970 interview, seventy-four-year-old Freeman Bennett remarked, "[I]n the nights ya know, long nights in the winter, well uh . . . they'd start tellin those stories an' _ pass away the time, that's all the pastime they had them times is tellin stories an' singin songs see" (Halpert and Widdowson 1996:623; transcription conventions theirs[3]). Children of all ages seem to have been allowed to stay up listening, as long as they were quiet (Barter 1979), though the tales were not necessarily directed at them.

For the male narrators of the male-centered tales of this collection, however, the pre-eminent context was the predominantly male world of the lumber camp, the fishing or sealing trip, or some other occupational endeavor. When Freeman Bennett was twenty-five years old and working on a bridge-building crew, he learned "Peter and Minnie" (AT 304) from Eli Roberts, a man fifteen years his senior: " . . . every time we'd go to our dinner _ he'd tell us a story see" (Halpert and Widdowson 1996:74). But Freeman and other narrators recall hearing and learning particular tales from older men at much earlier ages, too: as a "small kid" (10), "eight or nine year old" (501), "just a kid about age ten" (311). Typical of the male occupational context is Albert Heber Keeping's introduction to "The Queen of Paradise' Garden": "[I was] on a fishin voyage in . . . in Connaigre Bay. I was a boy o' twelve _ an' I was cook. An' after the day's work was finished those old _ men would tell up some old yarns, ghost stories _ an' so forth _ and one I kind o' remember _ more distinctly than others" (315). Several storytellers also remember more personal and private storytelling events in which a father or uncle narrated just to them (311): Everett and Freeman Bennett would visit their widower uncle on Saturday nights. All three would lie on the floor by the stove and the older man told stories until the boys, eight and eleven years old, fell asleep (494, 501).

Given that so many of the narrators in the collection recall learning tales from older men when they themselves were boys or teenagers, it seems likely that children and young adults were key audiences for the magic tale. In 1966, Allan Oake (not more than twenty when he learned his stories) claimed that a few men still came and asked for a story, and that they were "young fellers" (Halpert and Widdowson 1996:304), as opposed to old men like himself. Narrators' memories of male-to-male storytelling seem to support the idea that many Newfoundland Jack tales instructed young men and boys in how to be proper men according to the canons of working-class behavior: how to find and keep work, deal with adversarial employers, manage relations with parents, siblings, and elders, and, finally, meet a partner and future wife. In this sense, the tales were occupational narratives that showed "youngsters" how to be. What follows is an identification of the most prominent characteristics of Jack as a role model for young working men.

Jack as Role Model

Guarding knowledge

In Newfoundland, a striking trait of Jack's behavior is that he is circumspect in what he reveals about himself to anyone in authority. In Stephen Snook's tale "Greensleeves" (AT 313), Jack, the boy promised to an ogre, meets a series of three old men (potential donors) on his journey to find Greensleeves, the magician. The role of donor in a tale is to test the hero's worthiness to receive the helpful advice or magical gift that will enable him to succeed in his quest (Propp 1968:79). After giving the first old man a shave (they are all exceedingly whiskery), he admits that he *is* looking for Greensleeves. He is directed to the second brother, but there he denies knowing the first one: "'(Your) other brother' Jack said 'who's he?'" (Halpert and Widdowson 1996:83). And the same denial occurs with the third: Jack shaves him—an action that may symbolize a trusting relationship— but still denies knowing the others:

> "Well now" he said "John my son" he said _ "I got the most enchantment. I got two more brothers way back from this."
> Jack said "You('ve) two brothers have 'ee? (There're) a lot o' yous in family 'cordin (to) that!" (Halpert and Widdowson 1996:84)

Then the storyteller, in an aside, says confidentially: "He knew it all (fine but) he wouldn't tell un" (84). Such moments of metanarration bring the tale world and the real world briefly together. This is the moment when the narrator slips across the message to the youngsters in the audience that when confronted by someone with superior status and power—"enchantment"—you don't tell all your business; instead, you guard your knowledge. In the tale world all three old men have magic, but in real world terms they could represent the usual range of elders who might help a boy on his way up—if carefully dealt with.

This trait is re-emphasized later in this tale (as in other versions of AT 313 in the collection) when Jack denies he has received help from Greensleeves's daughter. Jack's denials to the donors prefigure his denials to the magician:

> "Daughter Ann" Jack said "what's that (a) cat? A dog or what is it?"
> "No" he said "my oldest daughter."
> "(Why)" he said "I didn't know you **HAD** any daughters" Jack [said].
> (Halpert and Widdowson 1996:90)

One of the real world messages of this tale may be *know whom to trust.* Once he has shaved the old men and gotten their instructions, Jack follows their words to the letter. As he approaches the pond where the ogre's daughters are swimming (in bird form), the narrator gives us Jack's interior monologue as he recalls the last old man's words: "'You [do] like he tells 'ee' he said 'an boy' he says 'you should come out of it alright.'" Jack walks on, then recalls, "'Now th' ol' man said

there was a pond too.' Sure enough Jack looked on, there was a pond."
The story progresses: "'Now,' Jack said, 'that wouldn't be his three
daughters off swimmin' would it?' Jack said. [Unidentified listener:
Hm!] 'Like th' ol' man told us, my gad,' he said, 'now it could be'"(86).

Jack has to choose carefully from the three piles of clothes the
girls left on the bank; he finds the satin dress that the old man has
told him to seize and not give up until the girl promises to take him
to her father:

> . . . "it's fairly /glistenin/. I couldn't hardly look at un, satin. Well now"
> Jack says "that's what . . . ol' man is right. I'LL be right." (Halpert and
> Widdowson 1996:86)

If this is a tale world modeling of real world behavior the moral is
clear: once a trusting relationship is made—with older men as advi-
sors or eventually with the loved one as partner—follow proffered
advice completely.

This principle of guarding one's knowledge is tied in to occupational status and reputation. In the early 1970s, during a life history
study that I made of Les Fussell, a retired farmworker from Bridport,
Dorset, he took pains to tell me that in his experience knowledge was
a property that had to be acquired by a process akin to theft, since in
the competitive working-class labor market a man's economic and
social worth depended on his exclusive possession of certain abilities
(Lovelace 1975:43). Gardeners, for example, "used to *guard* their
knowledge" (198), and men who could cure horses, as Les could,
were exceptionally valuable. When Les cured a horse that the veteri-
narian had failed to help, the farmer asked:

> "Leslie, what did you use?" [Note the formality of address: it is "Leslie"
> not "Les"—as Newfoundland ogres address Jack as "John"] And I said
> [matching formality in reply], "Mr. Huxter, if I told you, you would be
> as clever as me." (198)

This tussle between master and man over secret knowledge reminds
me of the culmination of the tasks sequence in "Greensleeves," where
the magician, finding that Jack seems to have comparable magic,
decides to kill him (note the formal address again):

> "Well John" he said "my son sorry to say" he said "but your head got
> to go on a spear" he said "in two hours from the day."
> "What!" Jack said. "After doin everything."
> "Yes" he said. "We tries 'em out" he said "of all kinds" he said "an'
> when they does . . . they sees that you got just so much enchantment as

we got ourself we makes away with 'em quick. You see all them heads on
the spears what's around here." He said "That's what uh . . . we been
(doin)." (Halpert and Widdowson 1996:93)

So knowledge is a guarded possession in the real world as in the tale
world. As Les told me when I tried to get deeper into his knowledge
of healing by charms, "Well, Martin, I'll tell you the way to learn. You
pick the brains of someone whose brains you can pick but there will
be some that you'll never pick. Shall we leave it like that?" (Lovelace
1975:43). I was rebuffed, but I kept my head.

Being Useful

The presentation of self shown by Jack in Newfoundland, and by working men in rural England, also includes a display of indifference to
personal pain and an emphasis on being sturdily, practically useful. In
England the good horseman or cowman puts his livestock first: the
animals are the center of his thought. This core value of the West Country farming community is voiced by a Newfoundland Jack in "The Blue
Bull," by Allan Oake (AT 511A+650A+300). Once again Jack is circumspect, keeping his giant-killing and princess-saving business secret from
the farmer's wife, at whose place he works as a cowman. When she tells
him of a girl to be "burned to death _ five hundred mile _ across another country," Jack says he is not interested. According to the narrator, "Wasn't interested he said [in] that at all. 'Twas . . . get a . . . feed
for his cows _ all he was interested in" (Halpert and Widdowson
1996:258). Generations of West Country cowmen would have approved
this sentiment and style of self-presentation.

Formal education, however, was viewed with suspicion in both English and Newfoundland working-class cultures; it was considered to make
a man unfit, or disinclined, for "real" work. In the "Hard Head" stories
(cf. AT 611 [Irish by-form]) Jack hides his good education and pre-
tends to be a dunce at school. As part of a larger duplicity, he hides the
fact that he and the rich girl, or princess, were married as infants, until
it suits him to reveal it after he has outwitted a rival suitor of higher
social class—a mayor or a duke. In these tales he allows the girl, as
Partner, to support and sponsor him. She puts him through school
(which leads to a job in her father's office) and outfits him with ships
as a merchant trader. Jack allows her to think him just a poor boy,
though it's established at the start that he is her social equal. Neither

does he tell her about the wager at the boarding house, where he loses his ships to a nefarious old woman who bets that Jack can go to bed with her daughter, or daughters, without "knowing what they are." The old woman drugs him, and only on the third time, with advice from a man he has helped, does Jack succeed in carnally knowing the daughters and winning back his ships. Nothing of this bet is revealed to the faithful sweetheart at home, of course; the double-standard goes unremarked by teller or characters and is quietly absorbed by the listening men. As contemporary athletes say about the sexual opportunities on road trips: "What happens on the road, stays on the road."

Newfoundland Jack does not always confide in his female Partner. In "Jack and the Goose" (AT 1536A), thanks to a grateful dead man, he gets to shore after being set adrift by the treacherous captain who abducted Jack and the girl:

> [H]e went over to the . . . king's house, he knocked to the door. An' the king's daughter come out an' opened the door. An' soon as she opened the door _ well she knowed Jack.
>
> "Oh" *[tones of hushed surprise]* she said "come in, come in" she said "Jack, come in." She [s]aid "Ey . . . ey . . . how . . . how di . . . how did you get here Jack?"
>
> "Oh" he said "I got here." Huh! *[laughs]*
>
> "Well" she said "come in." (Halpert and Widdowson 1996:754)

Jack preserves the mystique of his omni-competence, even with his trusting partner.

Deceiving words

Words are always mistrusted by those who doubt their capacity to use them safely, especially in the context of labor bargains. "Jack and the Duke" (AT 921) is built entirely around riddling, duplicitous answers to a series of questions. The duke agrees to pay Jack for any trick Jack can pull on him: Jack makes a fire on a barren rock by burning "lies and truth"—a newspaper. He literalizes metaphors: slashing the sides of rich men's horses in a stable, he says they split their sides laughing. He is fired for procuring a black woman to sleep with the duke, rather than the white one requested. He gets his job back by blackmailing the duke with the threat of telling his wife, but Jack actually tells her the duke fired him for bringing him a black chicken instead of a white one, and he is taken back into service. This riddling play with words bears out Stanley Brandes, who argues, in *Metaphors of Masculinity,* that Spanish peasant men are socialized into a basically skeptical attitude toward authority and labor bargains by playing at riddles, which focus attention on the deceptiveness of words and agreements (1980:136). Employers and other masters in the real world may be as capricious and arbitrary as posers of riddles by changing terms midway through a job. Greensleeves is the perfect example of the employer who continually adds to the tasks by which he holds Jack in thrall.

In terms of *how to be,* the Newfoundland tales advise young men to trust older men's advice, as well as the advice of their sweethearts and wives, who are likely to be more clever than they are. Labor bargains often are shown to be deceitful. Young men are told to guard their knowledge and say no more than necessary about their business to anyone, lest this information give others power over them. (The exact amount of any fisherman's catch—when there were still fish to be had—was a delicate matter, never precisely stated.) By adhering to these tacit real world principles Jack succeeds in the magic tale.

Not flinching

A further principle of the laboring man's self-presentation is never to admit that a task is too hard and never to seem to "flinch." The writer most attuned to this working-class dictum is George Sturt ("George Bourne"), the English author whose books about "Frederick Bettesworth," a Surrey laborer who would have been born in the 1840s, are masterpieces of intuitive ethnography (1901, 1907). Bettesworth refuses to accept help with a heavy load:

> . . . my mate, he knowed how my leg was, an' so when I come for my last bag he says, "Now look 'ere," he says, "if I sees you go to lift that up on your back, I shall knock 'n off again." "If you do," I says, "I shall knock ye down." And so I should. . . . "No," I says, "it's my turn and I en't gwine to flinch." "I knows you don't want to flinch," he says, "but I don't mind doin' of it for *you.*" And the foreman standin' there says, "No, old Fred've worked pole-pullin' 'long o' me thirty year, and I never knowed 'n flinch yet." "No," I says, "and I ben't gwine to now." But never no more, not another year . . . not if I en't got nothin' better 'n taters to live off from . . . " (Bourne 1901:324).

To be known to have flinched would have meant losing his place in the competitive labor market.

Newfoundland Jacks likewise refuse to admit anything is beyond their capacity. In responding to giants, magicians, and farmers, Jack consistently makes light of frightening, difficult, or laborious work. His presentation of self is as the all-capable worker, keen to tackle anything: "it's no trouble for me to kill **THAT** cat," says Jack, when acting as marksman for a giant (Halpert and Widdowson 1996:37); "only a few rats knockin about the house"—after a night in a haunted building (206). He chooses a rusty scythe over a new one: " 'cause if I had the best one I mow **TOO** much" (280). This trait occurs most markedly in the versions of AT 313, The Girl as Helper in the Hero's Flight. Jack's confident self-presentation is featured by each of the six narrators who tell this tale. In one version—after retrieving a needle from a barn full of manure—Jack tells the Green Man of Eggum, "'I was only a couple o' **HOURS'** he said 'gettin that out'" (124). Other narrators of AT 313 include similar scenes:

> "Did ya do (it?)" [the boss asks in No. 9, 136] "(Oh) yes" he said "an' so much more if I had to do."

> "Oh" . . . Jack said _ done perfect." (No. 10, 145)

> "Oh" he said "the best kind" he said "no problems at all." He said "Everything worked perfect." (No. 10, 146)

> "Oh! That's no trouble" Jack said. "Not much trouble to catch a . . . horse I don't suppose an' break un in." (No. 11, 151)

Jack lets down his guard and gives way to despair only when he is outside the competitive male arena and alone with the ogre's daughter. She feeds him, or gives him a magical implement, and coaxes him back to his tasks. Given that Newfoundland outport men did rely heavily on their wives to run the household, tend the livestock and garden, help "make" the salt fish, and keep the books for the family fishery, this relationship of dependency by the man on the woman's superior knowledge is an accurate picture of domestic life. The girl as helper defeats her ogre father by using her stronger magic to protect her husband. Barbara Rieti's fieldwork finds a significant parallel in the witch legends of contemporary Newfoundland (1995): one of the markers of witch behavior is to be a woman married to an ineffectual husband, for whom she constantly bullies others for favors and work. Presumably this threatens the male facade of authority, toughness, and competence which even the magic tales encourage men to maintain. Jack is dependent on the ogre's daughter, but he must not show this to the ogre or anyone else. Not that he should be a braggart—"self brag was scandal," one teller observes—but he must stick up for himself. These were some of the lessons in *how to be* that were available to listening boys.

The tales of several narrators in the collection seem to agree that Jack is stubborn and obstinate in his dealings with his master. A southern English vernacular phrase for this kind of unflinching demeanor is "being orkard." It comes from a 1938 book by Barclay Wills that reports interviews with Sussex shepherds. Strangers to this English county, writes Wills, often find people hard to deal with:

> [they] . . . will refuse for some obscure reason to answer a simple question, and say, afterwards, "I wasn't going to have *my* brains picked." . . . Some people are saddled with a further inheritance—a willful and masterful disposition, which makes them very aggressive. I have heard this trait referred to as "orkardness"; to many it is a virtue—a sign of great strength of character. People put up with an "orkard" man and respect him, whereas the stranger shuns him as he would a dog with a surly temper. (1938:27)

What Wills has noticed is not so much the characteristic of a county but a trait of a social class—the rural poor from whom so many workers in the Newfoundland fisheries were recruited. Here is Newfoundland Jack being "orkard": [he] "looked up, here was a **TWO** headed giant comin down. Come down over where Jack was an' . . . begin to mutter about those cows an' Jack said 'If you've anything to say' he said 'say it to **ME** not to the cows'" (Halpert and Widdowson 1996:257).

The giant could be any surly West Country farmer coming to find fault with his cowman. In the working world this is the kind of conflict recounted among farm workers as a confrontation narrative (Lovelace 1979). In such stories a man describes how he quarreled with his master over some perceived slight. The confrontation sometimes flares into telling the boss what he can do with his job. In the world of the Newfoundland magic tale Jack swings his five-hundred-pound iron cane and kills the giant. Both real world and tale world narrative endings are deeply cathartic.

Jack is orkard again in Allan Oake's "The Head Card Player of the World" (AT 313C), in which he is made to sleep with the pigs, then with the hens. After each night the master maliciously asks how he liked it. Jack will not give him the satisfaction of admitting that it was unpleasant:

> "Now" he said "how do ya like . . . last night . . . sleepin with a pig?"
> "Well" he said he could manage . . . he managed it alright.
> . . . "How 'ee's like to sleep wi' th' hens?"
> "Well" he said "not bad." (Halpert and Widdowson 1996:161)

On the third night the magician gives him a woman to sleep with:

> "Now how ya like . . . wi' woman to bed wi' ya?"
> "Not very good sir" he said. He said "I wasn't in bed very long after
> **SHE** got there." (162)

The principle is to be contrary: never give in to the master's whimsical bullying.

Jack's obduracy reaches its zenith in a tale called "The Cuckoo" by Freeman Bennett. It is a contest between master and man as to which of them will first admit to being "sorry." The first to weaken must take two cuts across the back with a big knife. Bill and Tom both fail in the first task they are set: to mow all the hay that the farmer's little dog (called a "cracky" in Newfoundland) can run over in a day. When Jack begins to mow the dog runs past and Jack "chopped his legs off. An' the cracky falled down an' _ Jack mowed uh . . . just what the cracky runned over an' he chucked down the scythe an' _ he never mowed no more" (Halpert and Widdowson 1996:620).

Jack goes home in the evening and tells the master what he has done:

> "[I] mowed what he runned over" he said uh . . . "an' I wouldn't mow
> no more."
> "Oh my!" he said "Jack" he said "you've aruined me!"
> "Well the devil might care!" Jack said "He had no business runnin
> around where I was mowin!" He [Jack] said "Is ya sorry?"
> "No" the ol' man said "I'm not sorry." (Halpert and Widdowson
> 1996:621)

Jack continues to whittle down the ogre's property, cutting out sheep eyes and throwing them when told to keep an eye on the master, and burning the house down when told to warm it. Jack's term of employment is not up until the cuckoo calls (an obvious survival of an English reference, since cuckoos aren't found in Newfoundland). To trick Jack into leaving, the farmer's wife climbs into a tree and "crows" like a cuckoo. Knowing full well what is going on, Jack throws a rock at the supposed bird and kills her. He tells the ogre,

"That wasn't a cuckoo at **ALL** you had up there!" He said "Is you sorry?"

He said "Yes" he said "I'm sorry." Well Jack took the big knife an' he killed un. An Jack took all his money an' he went home an'_ he had money enough. So they never tricked Jack then. *[laughs]*

The World They Left: English Peasant Antecedents of Newfoundland's Settlers

This savage humor may make a bourgeois reader queasy. Halpert's notes show how widespread this tale is as an international trickster story, so it would obviously be unwise to tie it specifically to a New-foundland or even English social background. Peasants everywhere have enjoyed this compensatory fantasy of revenge upon malicious and violent masters; Richard Chase's tale "Big Jack and Little Jack" is an American example (1943:67–75). Nevertheless, if this tale were not a fantasy—part of a tale world—Jack's character would be an ac-curate modeling of the kind of personality that historian G. R. Quaife describes as typical in English peasants between 1500 and 1800: "[T]he childhood of most peasants, separated from their parents at an early age and subjected to brutal discipline, produced cruel, cold, and sus-picious adults liable to outbursts of aggressive hostility towards each other. . . . the average peasant was a short-tempered, malicious char-acter who flared into physical violence on the flimsiest excuse" (Quaife 1979:25). This study of Somerset peasants in the seventeenth century is based on depositions in secular and ecclesiastical court proceed-ings. To the obvious charge that these documents will only show dis-turbances of the normal peace of everyday life, Quaife points out that such courts, in fact, inquired into "almost every aspect of human endeavour" and gathered evidence throughout the village commu-nity. He argues that these sources are among the few from which "the activities and attitudes of the largely illiterate lower orders can be discerned" (1979:v).

From such social historical accounts it becomes apparent that sepa-ration from family at an early age was not merely a fictional convention of the magic tale, nor was it only the high mortality rate that led to the stock depiction of cruel step-parents in the tales. Rather, in England at least, these tale world patterns had real world origins in the habit of "fostering out" children. Describing Somerset again Quaife says:

The typical household consisted of two parents, their children, and their servants. These servants or apprentices were often the children of neighbors, fostered out usually between the age of seven and twelve. They replaced some of the family's own children who had been sent to another household. Mutual fostering-out of children, sometimes from a very early age, may have been a major factor in the social and psychological development of the individual in this period. (1979:15)

The Newfoundland magic tale, like its English counterpart, has boys and girls going out to seek service and being maltreated by stepmothers or farmer's wives who load them with tasks, starve them, and spy on them. In his study of English migration to Newfoundland, the geographer W. Gordon Handcock quotes a Newfoundland planter's letter asking for "some hard boys with bone and health" to be shipped to him "for three summers and two winters" as indentured apprentices in his fishery at Newfoundland (1989:208–09). Such boys were often orphans or the children of people who made up the surplus agricultural population. Supervisors of parish relief in Dorset, Devon, and Somerset were glad to send away these charges to the local taxpayers. The youth promised to an ogre is the theme of the commonest tale in the collection, recorded from six tellers from all round the island (AT 313). In three other tales a boy, in one case specified as the poorest of boys (Halpert and Widdowson 1996:1002), is sought by a high-status male as an apprentice (Nos. 15, 149, 150); in one of these a sea captain is sent to abduct him, and abductions by captains occur in other tales, too (Nos. 21, 22, AT 506B; 53, AT 888*; 96, AT 1536A+AT 506B). In Freeman Bennett's "Little Jack," the boy comes up on deck and finds himself out of sight of land with no way of telling his grandmother what has happened to him (1015). When Jack sets off to find Greensleeves, the magician who holds him captive, and is given food by his mother and Nine Mile Boots by his father, with advice from old men about how he will have to tip footmen at each door leading to Greensleeves, it is easy to imagine a poor boy tramping away from Marnhull in agricultural North Dorset to the port town of Poole where he is to sign up as an apprentice with some wealthy man in the Newfoundland trade. Or he might be an outport youth on his way to St. John's on business with some politician, or a fisherman trying to settle his account with his merchant, trying to get "clear" (93). Real worlds and tale worlds coincide at such points, confirming Holbek's thesis that "symbolic elements in magic tales are emotional impressions of beings, phenomena and events in the real world, organized in the form of fictional narrative sequences which allow the narrator to speak of the problems, hopes and ideals of the community" (1987:435).

Conclusion

Roger DeV. Renwick suggests that "surprise value" should be one of the results of structural or semiotic analysis: patterns uncovered were not predicted and go against or add to previous understandings (1980:11). The surprise in the present investigation is the remarkable number of references to farmers and farming in *Folktales of Newfoundland*. Anyone who knows Newfoundland's cold, wet, stony, boggy, forested terrain knows that farming is not widespread or easy. The Codroy Valley on the west coast does have pastures and hayfields; so too do areas south of St. John's. In the past, outport families were far more self-reliant in growing vegetables than they are currently, and they kept cows, goats, sheep, and hens, along with horses for work in the woods. Perhaps this small-scale semi-subsistence farming is what tellers have in mind. But it is unlikely that a Jack setting out on a day's march would find a farmer's house conveniently at the end of each day, as he certainly would in Dorset, Normandy, Britanny, or County Cork. What we may have in the implicit backgrounds of the Newfoundland folktales is a kind of scrim: a thin curtain of Newfoundland adaptations and references through which the landscape of the old countries can still be glimpsed. In the explicit foreground Jack sits down to boil his kettle, as any Newfoundland hunter or berrypicker would, while his horse sucks up enough water to douse a fiery dragon, but the farm he left that morning and to which he will return is the Somerset or Dorset farm where he is the backhouse boy under the heel of some termagant farmwife.

Using a word-search program, I assembled all the references in the book to farming and fishing respectively.[4] Eighteen tales alluded to farming directly; at least one more involved it without using the word. In seven tale types from six tellers, Jack (or his wife) gets work on a farm. In four separate tales Jack is a farmer's son. Fishing occurs in only two tales and in one of these it is called "trouting" rather than being the industrial codfishery that sustained Newfoundland for four hundred years. While the tales mention boatbuilding, voyages, and hardbread, there is also a striking retention of a rural agricultural scene and perhaps a similar set of attitudes. As one who grew up in the West of England I recognize in the tales an attitude toward farmers that I know from my own family tradition and from men who worked on farms in Dorset: farmers are skinflints, reputedly rich, apparently mean. Freeman Bennett's "Jack Lives Without Eating" satirizes the traditional eccentric parsimony of farmers. The man is delighted to hire Jack, because he says he can live without food. The farmer muses,

> "Well" he said "Jack" he said "I'd like to be able to give up eatin." He said "If I . . . I could give up eatin" he said "I'd save a lot more money." (Halpert and Widdowson 1996:841)

In Stephen Snook's "A Ship Sailed On Wind and Water," the problem between master and man is that the farmer does not bring Jack any dinner. When the farmer and his wife inspect the field Jack has mown they find he has traded away the crop to a supernatural figure who paid him in magical food.

For a culture that regards itself as quintessentially marine, the prominence of farming in the narratives is a surprise. Have insufficient generations elapsed to scrub out the idea of farmers as autocratic adversaries of working men? The ancestors of most Newfoundlanders in their "old countries" were not sailors and fishermen but agricultural laborers. Are these retentions in the tales signs of a greater conservatism than we might have expected: passing on the tale as it was heard? Do the tales preserve a seventeenth- or eighteenth-century English peasant's attitude to work and employers? Or is it that the disjunction between the idea of an eighty-acre hayfield and the acre or so that would have been more normal in Newfoundland simply fits the unreality of the magic tale, and so is retained as fantasy? Pius Power, a great Newfoundland tale teller whose stories unfortunately do not appear in *Folktales of Newfoundland*, sometimes used the following opening formula:

> Well there was one time
> in olden times
> 'twas in farmer's times
> 'twasn't in your time or in my time
> but in times ago. (Best 1988:43)

Anita Best, who has recorded many of his tales,[5] found that Märchen were the very last stories told on an evening that typically had begun with gossip about the day's work. Perhaps in Newfoundland farmers have become markers of the exotic, the outlandish, like the houses papered with pancakes in other formulas? Structural analysis indicates that they occupy the same narrative slot as kings, magicians, and giants, all arbitrary and autocratic figures of power but distanced from everyday experience.

The magic tale is too rich and complex a form to be reduced to any single explanation. *Folktales of Newfoundland* provides material for many contending or complementary interpretations. Here I have argued that, among other things, the tales were primers to boys on how to carry themselves in the working world. From this angle they could be oral equivalents of the "Letter of Advice to a Son," which Lawrence Stone describes as a common moral and literary exercise among the English landed classes of the seventeenth century. These writings, assuming a contemporary world of casual violence and mutual suspicion, advised that the "only safe way to manoeuvre through the world is by the exercise of extreme self-control, outward reserve, secrecy, and even duplicity" (1977:96). Some of the Newfoundland Jacks seem to act on exactly these principles. Whether the picture of antagonistic and deceptive social relations seen in the Newfoundland tales is in any way a retention of an earlier English worldview is a subject too large to be broached here. The textual evidence, however, may suggest that the tales hold two views of society simultaneously: one, of a dangerous world of powers wielded by unpredictable autocrats—adversarial employers of a higher social class; the other, of a warm, hospitable, familial world of helpful older men—donors, in Propp's terminology, who send the youth further on his search, ultimately to meet the resourceful, constant, female partner. These two perspectives would represent, respectively, the world of work and the world of home. The Newfoundland tales are "workers' literature" (Holbek 1987:607) imbued with a regional history of class exploitation and antagonism. Using Halpert and Widdowson's remarkable new resource and following Holbek's insights, we can move beyond presumptuous attribution of universal symbolism to tales and instead try to approach their regionally and historically conditioned meanings.

Memorial University of Newfoundland
St. John's

Notes

1. This example from the *Oxford Dictionary of English Proverbs* (1970:408) expresses the assertive attitude in defense of working men's rights that I will argue to be one of the lessons taught to young Newfoundland men by these tales.

2. I am deeply grateful to John Widdowson and the late Herbert Halpert for encouraging me to present a version of this essay at the American Magic Conference at the University of Houston in October 1997. My participation was supported in part by the Canadian Consulate General, Dallas.

I also thank Carl Lindahl, General Editor of Garland's World Folktale Library, first for imagining the conference and bringing it about, and then for his kind invitation to Houston as part of the launching of *Folktales of Newfoundland*. While I assisted with aspects of the book from 1976 onward I did not take part in the fieldwork, and my comments are no more than inferences. Whatever errors and misinterpretations I have made are my own. Thanks for useful editorial suggestions are also extended to the anonymous reviewer(s) of this essay.

3. In passages quoted from Halpert and Widdowson, the following typographic conventions were used:

[ ] Brackets have four functions:
(a) enclosing brief editorial interventions;
(b) denoting reconstructions of muffled or semi-inaudible forms, the reconstructions being preceded by a question mark if tentative;
(c) identifying speech by the interviewer or others present;
(d) marking the narrator's asides to the audience.

( ) Parentheses denote tentative transcriptions of unclear speech, conjectural transcriptions being preceded by a question mark.

/ / Slant lines mark the substitution of corrected forms for misencodings, conjectural substitutions being preceded by a question mark. . . .

. The period usually denotes a pause following a falling intonation at the end of an utterance or following a distinctive rising tone requesting agreement. Occasionally the period is used, like the comma, to signify a sense break before the transition to a new idea, but only if a brief pause is detectable (otherwise a comma is used). The use of the period is often justified by an intonational shift following a minimal pause. When the speech flows on without a pause, the period is not used.

, The comma is used to separate segments of speech for syntactical clarity and to resolve possible ambiguity where phrases are run together in speech without a pause and the sense of the utterance may be unclear when transferred to print; it does not indicate a pause. Its positioning is often suggested by a shift of vocal tone demarcating a pivotal change from "end of thought" to "transition to a new idea."

_ The single underlining symbol, preceded and followed by a space, notes a brief pause, often for breath.

. . . Three ellipsis points represent a brief pause preceding correction or re-encoding of a false start, usually involving hesitation. . . .

Boldface Denotes strong emphasis. (Halpert and Widdowson 1996:lxii–lxiii)

4. Here I gratefully acknowledge the help of Mrs. Eileen Collins, the truly indispensable member of the book's team, who produced its camera-ready copy and undertook this word search for me.

5. Anita Best, "Female Characters in Newfoundland *Märchen,*" part of her monograph in progress on Pius Power and his storytelling.

References Cited

Apo, Satu
1995   *The Narrative World of Finnish Fairy Tales.* Folklore Fellows Communications No. 256. Helsinki: Academia Scientiarum Fennica.

Barter, Geraldine
1979   "The Folktale and Children in the Tradition of French Newfoundlanders." *Canadian Folklore Canadien* 1:5–11.

Best, Anita
1988   "Female Characters in Newfoundland *Märchen.*" Unpublished paper.

Bourne, George [George Sturt]
1901   *The Bettesworth Book: Talks with a Surrey Peasant.* London: Duckworth.
1907   *Memoirs of a Surrey Labourer: A Record of the Last Years of Frederick Bettesworth.* London: Duckworth.

Brandes, Stanley
1980   *Metaphors of Masculinity: Sex and Status in Andalusian Folklore.* Philadelphia: University of Pennsylvania Press.

Buchan, David
1982   "Propp's Tale Role and a Ballad Repertoire." *Journal of American Folklore* 95:159–72.

Chase, Richard
1943   *The Jack Tales: Folk Tales from the Southern Appalachians.* Cambridge, Mass.: Houghton Mifflin.

Dégh, Linda
1969   *Folktales and Society: Story-telling in a Hungarian Peasant Community,* trans. Emily M. Schossberger. Bloomington: Indiana University Press.
1981   "The Peasant Element in the Hungarian and East European Magic Tale." *Cahiers de Litterature Orale* 9:45–77.

Desplanques, Marie-Annick
1985   *Folktales from Western Newfoundland.* Rouen: Université de Rouen.

Halpert, Herbert, and J. D. A. Widdowson
1996   *Folktales of Newfoundland: The Resilience of the Oral Tradition.* 2 vols. New York and London: Garland.

Handcock, W. Gordon
1989   *Soe longe as there comes noe women: Origins of English Settlement in Newfoundland.* St. John's: Breakwater.

Holbek, Bengt
1987   *Interpretation of Fairy Tales: Danish Folklore in a European Perspective.* Folklore Fellows Communications No. 239. Helsinki: Academia Scientiarum Fennica.

Lannon, Alice, and Michael McCarthy
1991   *Fables, Fairies & Folklore of Newfoundland.* St. John's: Jesperson Press.

Lovelace, Martin
1975   "The Life History of a Dorset Folk Healer: The Influence of Personality on the Modification of a Traditional Role." M.A. thesis, Memorial University of Newfoundland.
1979   "'We Had Words': Narratives of Verbal Conflicts." *Lore and Language* 3:29–37.
Murray, Hilda Chaulk
1979   *More Than Fifty Percent: Woman's Life in a Newfoundland Outport 1900–1950.* St. John's: Breakwater.
Nicolaisen, W. F. H.
1997   Review of *Folktales of Newfoundland*, by Halpert and Widdowson. *Newfoundland Studies* 13:93–97.
Ortutay, Gyula
1972   "Mihályi Fedics Relates Tales." *Hungarian Folklore: Essays.* Budapest: Akadémiai Kiadó, 225–85.
Propp, Vladímir
1968   *Morphology of the Folktale.* Austin: University of Texas Press.
Quaife, G. R.
1979   *Wanton Wenches and Wayward Wives: Peasants and Illicit Sex in Early Seventeenth Century England.* New Brunswick, N.J.: Rutgers University Press.
Renwick, Roger deV.
1980   *English Folk Poetry: Structure and Meaning.* Philadelphia: University of Pennsylvania Press.
Rieti, Barbara
1991   *Strange Terrain: The Fairy World in Newfoundland.* St. John's: Institute of Social and Economic Research.
1995   "Guns and Bottles: Newfoundland Counterwitchcraft Tactics as Assertions of Masculinity." *Folklore Interpreted: Essays in Honor of Alan Dundes*, ed. Regina Bendix and Rosemary Lévy Zumwalt, 167–82. New York: Garland.
Röhrich, Lutz
1991   *Folktales and Reality.* Trans. Peter Tokofsky. Bloomington: Indiana University Press.
Stone, Lawrence
1977   *The Family, Sex and Marriage in England 1500–1800.* London: Weidenfeld.
Thomas, Gerald
1983   *Les Deux Traditions: Le conte populaire chez les Franco-Terreneuviens.* Montréal: Bellarmin.
1993   *The Two Traditions: The Art of Storytelling Amongst French Newfoundlanders.* St. John's: Breakwater.
1997   "Early Life Crises and the Resolution of Conflict: Meaning in a Franco-Newfoundland Fairy Tale," *Newfoundland Studies* 13:153–77.
1999   "Recognizing Female Sexuality: AT 313, The Maid as Mentor in the Young Man's Maturation." *Estudos de Literatura Oral* (Universidade do Algarve) 5:161–69
Wills, Barclay
1938   *Shepherds of Sussex.* London: Skeffington.
Wilson, F. P., ed.
1970   *The Oxford Dictionary of English Proverbs.* 3d ed. Oxford: Clarendon Press.

In Memoriam: Herbert Halpert
1911–2000

WHEN HERBERT HALPERT died suddenly at home in St. John's, Newfoundland, on December 29, 2000, he was still awaiting the publication of his revised doctoral dissertation, completed in 1947, and several articles. The lengthy gestation period of many of Halpert's writings resulted from the detailed annotation he applied to all his work. (He was a master of comparative annotation; his notes to Vance Randolph's series of Ozark folktales, starting with *Who Blowed Up the Church House?* [1952], are particularly fine.) Halpert was thus not a prolific author in the manner of many of his generation, partly because of his desire to find every possible reference to a work and to incorporate it usefully into his text, and also because he was rarely satisfied with his editing of his own work. This explains why many of his articles and books were co-authored or received editorial attention from a colleague or from his wife, Violetta Maloney Halpert. He was a perfectionist, and this was nowhere more evident than in another of his strengths: teaching.

Halpert had the gift of inspiring students to discover, explore, and learn to appreciate their own culture. He developed this approach in a series of appointments to universities in Kentucky, Illinois, and New York, before joining the English department at the Memorial University of Newfoundland in 1962, where he would found the Department of Folklore, and its Folklore and Language Archive, in 1968. Most of the Memorial students who undertook graduate studies in folklore under his direction in the sixties and seventies went on to successful academic careers. They recall, sometimes with a wry grimace, the hours spent reading their thesis drafts aloud to him; the patient and attentive student eventually produced an eminently readable work, with careful annotations and some degree of originality. Halpert was no admirer of jargon, unless each term was first glossed in clear English. As his former students began teaching folklore, they were generally eager to pass on his experience and expertise to new generations.

If Halpert was not as prolific a writer as some of his peers (though his published books, articles, reviews, and annotations number close to one hundred and fifty, and his editorial work was immense), many of his publications were significant in their theoretical content. He became a "contextual-functionalist" long before the term was widely adopted. While a graduate student under Stith Thompson at Indiana University, Halpert bucked the trend by *not* producing a type or motif index as his dissertation. Instead, he focused on narratives and narrators from the New Jersey Pines, studying a living tradition of storytelling. He reported the aesthetic and evaluative comments of his informants on their own folklore in addition to recording their life histories, as later became standard practice. Halpert thus offered not only rich, fieldwork-based contexts in which to set his texts, but he also explored the functions of the folklore he collected—and was one of the very first folklorists to do so.

A summary of Halpert's career to 1980 appears in his Festschrift, *Folklore Studies in Honour of Herbert Halpert* (ed. Kenneth S. Goldstein and Neil V. Rosenberg, St. John's: Memorial University of Newfoundland). "Herbert Halpert: A Biographical Sketch," by Neil V. Rosenberg (pp. 1–13), is detailed and accurate; it is based on lengthy interviews with Halpert in which he ensured, with a careful annotator's eye, that all the important points of his career were noted and that appropriate credit was given where due. It is a biographical sketch that had the subject's approval. At this time, however, twenty more years of scholarship lay ahead of him, and he was particularly productive in his latter years. In 1982, *A Folklore Sampler from the Maritimes*—fruit of Halpert's year as the Winthrop Pickard Bell Professor of Maritime Studies at Mount Allison University (New Brunswick) in 1979–1980— was published, and his *magnum opus*, the two volume *Folktales of Newfoundland* (co-authored with J. D. A. Widdowson) appeared in 1996. Additionally some fourteen articles of greater and lesser significance were published after his 1980 Festschrift, with at least two more to appear posthumously.

Halpert received many honors in his career: he was elected a Fellow of the American Anthropological Society in 1954, Fellow of the American Folklore Society in 1960, Honorary Member of the Folklore Society (England) in 1974, and an Honorary President of the Folklore Studies Association of Canada in 1976. He was made Professor Emeritus by Memorial University in May 1979, following a six-year tenure as the Henrietta Harvey Professor of Folklore, a research chair. His greatest distinctions came, however, in the period between 1987 and 1994. In 1987 he was awarded a D. Litt by Memorial University; in 1989 he was elected an Honorary Member of the International Society for Folk-Narrative Research; and he received his second honorary degree, a D. Litt. from York University (Ontario), in 1990. In 1992 he was elected an Honorary Fellow of the Folklore Fellows (Finland), and in 1994 gained a third D. Litt., this time from the University of Sheffield (England). In April 1998, Halpert suffered a stroke, and although he made slow but steady progress in his recovery, he necessarily relied on the support of his wife and former colleagues to complete or advance his many unfinished projects.

Herbert Halpert will be remembered primarily as a scholar of folk narrative, but that is "narrative" as he himself used it, to include everything from potential narratives such as dites through the most complex of Märchen. Many of his most important articles deal with legends.

He wrote extensively on the legend, beginning with his doctoral dissertation. Local legends, witch legends, devil and the fiddle legends, place name legends, religious legends, legends of the Man-in-the-Moon, historical legends—all were grist for his mill. Most of his writings raise theoretical issues that had not generally surfaced before he took up the subject.

Halpert did not begin his career as a folk narrative specialist, however, but as a collector of children's rhymes and of folksongs. These genres, along with most others generally considered to be part of folklore, remained constant interests throughout his career. He felt that scholars who focused too narrowly on a single genre risked not understanding the interrelatedness of *all* the traditions in a given community. For instance, while working under the auspices of the WPA and as a member of its Joint Committee on Folk Arts, Halpert was chosen to record singers in several southern states whose songs had already been written down by workers on the Federal Writers' Project. During a trip that began in March 1939, Halpert not only recorded large numbers of "accepted" folksongs, but he also recorded much that had hitherto received little or no attention from folklorists: locally-composed songs, Black work songs, field calls, hollers, both Black and White religious singers, play-party songs, children's singing games, auctioneer chants, Black jail songs, and instrumental music. He noted that "by a lucky accident" he also recorded "long tales"—later to be known as "Jack tales"—from members of the Harmon family. (Halpert often told his students about this deceptively simple point: that singers might also know tales.) In a fourteen-week fieldtrip, he recorded 419 disks.

While a graduate student at Columbia University, Halpert had already decided that rather than study exotic societies he would use the anthropological approach to study folklore in North America. It was this approach that characterized Halpert's future research, writing, and teaching and set him apart from other folklorists of the day. Indeed it was not until the 1960s that "new" approaches, pioneered by Halpert, began to characterize a younger generation of folklore scholars.

These then are the principal hallmarks of Herbert Halpert's long and distinguished career: a vast bibliographical knowledge incorporated in all his work, often as eminently readable notes; rich and thoughtful annotations; provocative articles on a wide range of folkloristic topics, chiefly on narrative forms and types but also on folksong, folk language, custom, and belief; an extensive and important contribution to scholarship as editor of journals and books, in series or individually; and a remarkable gift for teaching, for guiding thesis and dissertation research, and for mentoring and advising colleagues in Folklore and other disciplines. It is unlikely there will be many scholars in younger generations with such a breadth of bibliographic knowledge and such extensive and intensive fieldwork experience. Halpert passed on his expertise willingly and generously, and those whose minds were open to it were by far the better scholars—and individuals—for it. He is sorely missed.

Gerald Thomas
Memorial University of Newfoundland
St. John's

Abstracts

CARL LINDAHL, Introduction: Representing and Recovering the British- and Irish-American Märchen

Throughout the twentieth century, folklorists devoted more energy to denying or downplaying the existence of the British- and Irish-American Märchen than to seeking out and learning from its narrators. This brief history of North American Märchen studies identifies some reasons for the academy's neglect of the genre, outlines the careers of the two early collectors (Vance Randolph and Leonard Roberts) most responsible for documenting oral Märchen traditions, and weighs the enormous influence of Richard Chase and his book *The Jack Tales* on both the academic community and the public at large. The essay also traces the efforts of Herbert Halpert and others to advance British- and Irish-American Märchen studies. It concludes by assessing important recent Märchen scholarship (as exemplified in books by William B. McCarthy, Charles L. Perdue Jr., and Herbert Halpert and J. D. A. Widdowson) and by describing the research of Perdue, Martin Lovelace, and Carl Lindahl included in this volume.

CARL LINDAHL, Sounding a Shy Tradition: Oral and Written Styles of American Mountain Märchen

Past literary critics of the Märchen defined the genre by identifying it in terms of a relatively small number of presumably universal traits. This study considers the extent to which the Märchen of the Appalachian and Ozark regions embody three of those "universals": 1) a perfectly memorable plot constructed to convey an invariant meaning; 2) sharp, bright, and sparse imagery; and 3) a tone of magical wonder. I examine the published tales of the regions' best-known collectors: Richard Chase, Leonard Roberts, and Vance Randolph. Comparing Chase's written renditions to the oral performances of Sam Harmon, I find that Chase misrepresents and undercuts the Märchen aesthetics of the family from whom he claimed to have gotten his tales. I examine Leonard Roberts's published versions of tales told by Jane Muncy and, considering the oral testimony and performances of the Muncy family, conclude that Roberts's tales are largely faithful to the tellers' oral styles. I end with an appreciation of Vance Randolph, whose tales demonstrate a regional tendency to treat the Märchen not as a tale of wonder, but as a legend or a joke. None of the three universals posited by literary scholars effectively characterizes the oral styles of the American mountain Märchen.

CHARLES L. PERDUE JR., Is Old Jack Really Richard Chase?

For many scholars and narrators, after Richard Chase published *The Jack Tales* in 1943 his name became synonymous with this type of narrative. Chase was an inveterate performer and told his collated versions of the tales throughout America; in some cases, he supplanted traditional tale tellers in their own communities. Though narrative scholars knew from the beginning that Chase's tales were bowdlerized compilations, original texts were not available for purposes of comparing and analyzing Chase's alterations. As a part of the WPA's Virginia Writers' Project, however, twenty-eight Jack tales were collected in Wise County, Virginia, in 1941 and 1942; these tales—unaffected by Chase's alterations—were discovered in the early 1980s. When analyzed in combination with the eleven Jack tales published by Isabel Gordon Carter in 1925, they make it possible to determine the nature of some changes made by Chase in his public presentations of "Jack tales." In this article, Perdue compares the distribution of particular traits in these published tales and determines that, in a number of ways, Richard Chase's Jack tales are less emblematic of the narrators he claimed to represent and more a reflection of himself.

MARTIN LOVELACE, Jack and His Masters: Real Worlds and Tale Worlds in Newfoundland Folktales

This essay argues that the male-centered Märchen of Halpert and Widdowson's *Folktales of Newfoundland* offer models of behavior for young working-class men, particularly in their relationships with employers. Close reading of the tales shows them to be lessons in life as seen from the perspective of a subordinated social class: they tell young men "how to be" in order to get employment and protect themselves from exploitation. Advice is also given regarding whom to trust and how to conduct love relationships. A further conclusion of the study is that for a quintessentially maritime culture, Newfoundland's magic tales refer surprisingly often to an agricultural world as their implicit background. It is suggested that this reflects a continuity of culture between Newfoundland and the areas in southeast Ireland and southwest England from which its settlers came. The transference of working-class modes of self-presentation from the West of England to Newfoundland is argued on the basis of personal fieldwork and published literature.

Contributors

JAMES TAYLOR ADAMS (1892–1954) was a largely self-educated man whose varied occupations included coal mining, sales, and library management. He published numerous articles about local history and folklore of the Cumberland Mountains and in the 1930s and '40s conducted research for a series of WPA cultural documentation projects. In 1941 Adams published *Death in the Dark: A Collection of Factual Ballads of American Mine Disasters, with Historical Notes;* his childhood memoir, *Grandpap Told Me Tales,* was published posthumously in 1993.

GLEN MUNCY ANDERSON, daughter of Sidney Farmer Muncy, was born in 1911 in Leslie Co., Kentucky. As a young girl, she listened to witch tales and jokes told by her grandmother, Rachel Wilson; in addition, her mother performed magic tales for her and her three siblings at bedtime. As an adult, Glen Muncy Anderson told many tales to her own children, though she did not retell the Märchen that she found frightening as a child. She now lives in Danville, Kentucky, with her younger sister Hope (b. 1916), who is also a fine storyteller.

RICHARD CHASE (1904–1988) grew up in Huntsville, Alabama. As a young man he became enamored with the idea of using folk narrative, song, and dance to teach contemporary children about their ostensible cultural past. Chase worked in schools and at festivals, and beginning in 1935 he spent much of his time collecting, revising, publishing, and performing magic tales that had roots in Appalachia. His publications include *The Jack Tales* (1943), *Grandfather Tales* (1948), and *American Tales and Songs* (1956).

JANE MUNCY FUGATE has been an avid storyteller since childhood, when her grandmother, Sidney Farmer Muncy of Leslie Co., Kentucky, taught her the art. Like her grandmother (a former teacher), Fugate has crafted tales to educate and entertain for decades. Her narratives have been anthologized in Leonard Roberts's *South from Hell-fer-Sartin* (1955) and *Old Greasybeard: Tales from the Cumberland Gap* (1969). She currently lives in Arizona.

177

SAMUEL HARMON (1870–1940) was born in Watauga Co., North Carolina. The son of John Goulder Monroe Harmon and Nancy Jane Hicks, he learned his folktales from his grandfather, "Little Sammy" Hicks (ca.1800–ca. 1880). Late in life, Samuel Harmon left North Carolina to live with his son, Austin, in Maryville, Tennessee, where he entertained Austin's children by telling tales, including narratives that he invented at their request. In April 1939, Herbert Halpert visited the home in Maryville and recorded Samuel Harmon performing fifteen tales.

POLLY JOHNSON was born in Pike Co., Kentucky, in 1865; from 1879 until at least 1939 she lived in Wise Co., Virginia, where she tended to her family of three, her four-room frame house, and her vegetable garden. Emory L. Hamilton of the WPA's Virginia Writers' Project reported that "numerous flower plants cluster[ed] in nearly every accessible place" in her tidy yard. Johnson was both a narrator and singer; Hamilton alone collected 31 songs from her. She was his favorite collaborator, having "the best voice and tune for the old folk-ballads."

ALICE LANNON grew up in Lawn, on the Burin Peninsula, Newfoundland; she has lived in various outport communities in Newfoundland and has also traveled widely beyond it. Her book, *Fables, Fairies and Folklore of Newfoundland*, co-written with her brother Michael McCarthy, appeared in 1991; this volume was followed by their *Ghost Stories from Newfoundland Folklore* in 1995.

CARL LINDAHL, Professor of English at the University of Houston, is series editor of the World Folktale Library. Among other publications, he has recently edited or authored several collaborative works: *Swapping Stories: Folktales from Louisiana* (1997), *Cajun Mardi Gras Masks* (1997), and *Medieval Folklore: An Encyclopedia* (2000). He is currently preparing an anthology of folktales from sound recordings housed in the American Folklife Center, Library of Congress.

MARTIN LOVELACE was born in Bridport, in southwest England. After earning degrees in English from the Universities of Wales and Alberta, he was introduced to the study of folklore by Herbert Halpert at Memorial University of Newfoundland and received the M.A. and Ph.D. under his supervision. He has taught at Memorial since 1980 and is currently Head of the Department of Folklore.

LOUISE FONTAINE MANN was born around 1885; sometime later, the Fontaine family left its Beaverdam Plantation in Hanover Co., Virginia, and moved to Charlottesville. Though one of her brothers attended college, Mann, her sister, and two brothers were largely home schooled. She married William Jackson Mann, an engineer and manufacturer, and had three children. According to her nephew C. E. "Chick" Moran Jr., Louise Fontaine Mann and her cousin Mary Willis Minor were known in the family as storytellers.

CHARLES L. PERDUE JR. worked for the U.S. Army Security Agency during the Korean War and for the U.S. Geological Survey before receiving a Ph.D. in Folklore from the University of Pennsylvania in 1971. Since then, he has taught courses in ethnohistory, life history, and folklore at the University of Virginia. Scholarly interests include Shenandoah National Park removals as well as southern narrative and music. He and Nancy J. Martin-Perdue edited *Talk About Trouble: A New Deal Portrait of Virginians in the Great Depression* (1996).